Exploring Denver Mountain Parks

A Guide To 22 Historic Getaways

by Mike Butler

On the cover-
Denver's Summit Lake Park reflects Mount Evans on a snowy
September day.

ISBN-13: 978-0615709628
ISBN-10: 0615709621

Published By:
Open Range Publishing
9415 Wolfe Place
Highlands Ranch, CO 80219

This book is dedicated to Lee Gylling and A.J. Tripp-Addison, retired Denver Mountain Park Superintendents. It was a pleasure working with these ardent supporters of Denver Mountain Parks.

A word about images and maps used in this book:
All images were photographed by the author or consist of historical items in the author's personal collection. Some photographs are of public signs in the Mountain Parks. Maps are public maps available from Denver Parks and Recreation, Denver Theaters and Arenas, Jefferson County Open Space, and the U.S. Forest Service.

Contents

Foreword

Echo Lake Park- A Denver Mountain Park located in Clear Creek County

"Not content with a distant view, Denver people have always gone into the mountains for recreation." (Louisa Ward Arps)

"No highway sign marks the entrance to Little Park near Idledale. When surveyed, a Denver resident says that he and his wife would visit Denver Mountain Parks if they only had any idea where they are." (Denver Mountain Parks Master Plan)

Not only is there no highway sign for Little Park, there is no highway sign for Starbuck Park, and there is no sign for Colorow Point Park. There are no information centers for Denver Mountain Parks with brochures or maps. But the Parks are there, and they are beautiful, majestic, peaceful, and yes, sometimes hidden. I discovered Little Park by hiking east from Jefferson County's Lair O' the Bear Park. I found that it had a lovely well house, picnic ground, and parking lot with a road leading down from the highway. Next trip I knew where to turn from the highway to Little Park. It took me three trips to find Starbuck Park and I was intentionally looking for it. This book aims to remedy those problems with specific directions and maps to all the developed parks, and guides of what to see and do in each park.

4

Colorow Point Park
Lookout Mountain Park
20
Brook
Bald Mtn. 9000'
Genesee Park
Katherine Craig Park
LOOKOUT MTN RD
Apex Park
ver
eek
Genesee Mtn. 8274'
Fillius Park
Green Mtn. 6900'
Mathews / Winters Park
Bergen Park
KERR GULCH RD
Starbuck Park
Bear Creek Canyon Park
Hogback Park
eadow
Corwina Park
Kittredge
Lair O' The Bear Park
Mt. Morrison 7878'
Bear Creek Canyon
Red Rocks Park
Morrison Park
Morrison
74
74
Creek
Little Park
O'Fallon Park
Soda Lake
9
Dedisse Park
Elephant Butte 8405'
Evergreen
Bear
Pence Park
Mt. Falcon 8100'
Mount Falcon Park
Mount Glennon
Alderfer / Three Sisters Park
Evergreen Mtn. 8800'
Dillon Park
Cub Creek Park
Bell Park
Bear Mtn. 8600'
INDIAN HILLS RD
Indian Hills
FOREST RD
73
Cub
BROOK
334
N TURKEY CREEK RD
Creek
Turkey
Turkey Creek Park
S TURKEY CREEK RD
Berrian Mtn. 9020'
Doublehead Mtn. 8800'
Bald Mtn. 7700'
124
Turkey
Creek
DEER CREEK CANYON
SHADOW MTN DR
Meyer Ranch Park
South
Legault Mtn. 9065'
Deer Creek Canyon P
Conifer

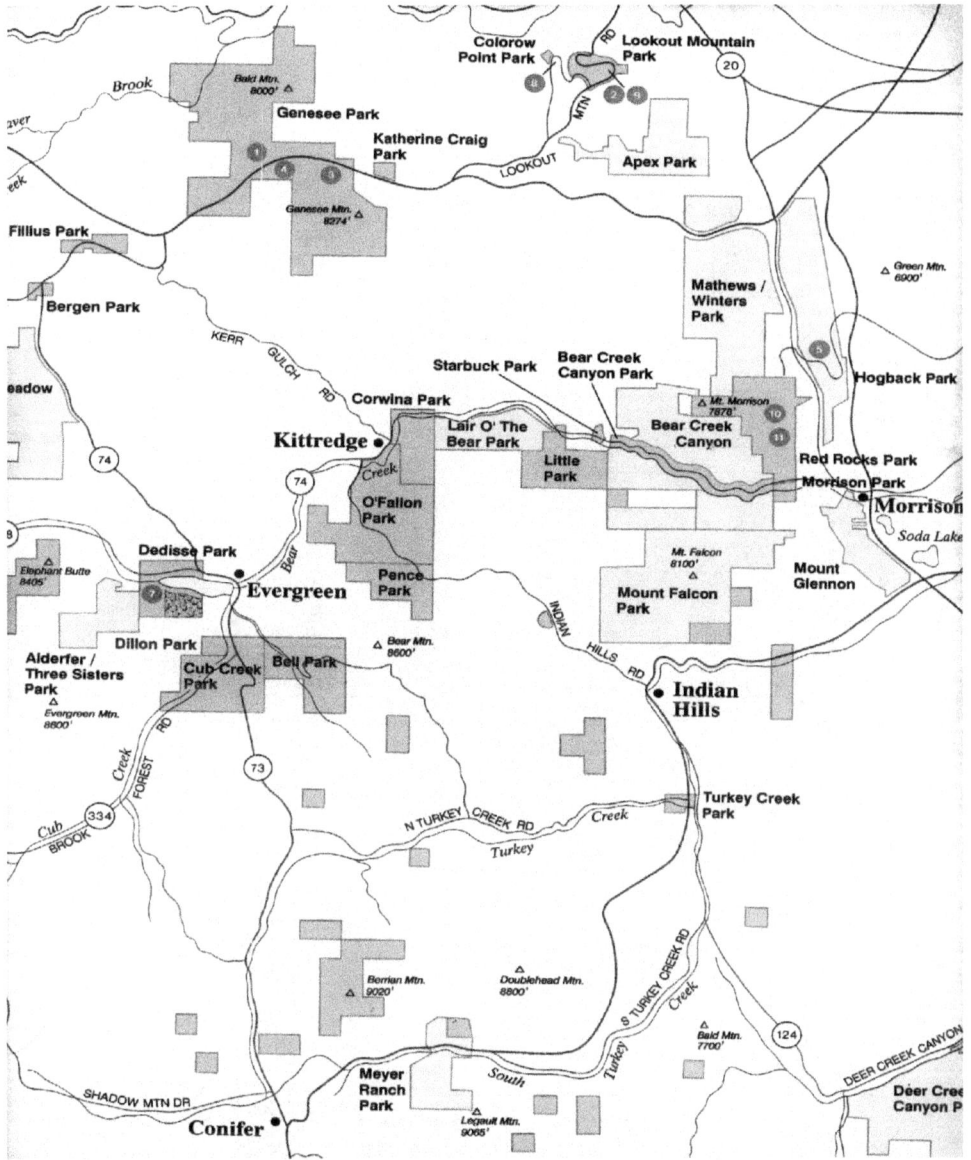

Denver Mountain Parks Location Map

Denver Mountain Parks are in dark gray and Jefferson County Open Space Parks are in light gray. Five parks are off the map- Newton Park is south of Conifer; Echo Lake and Summit Lake Parks are west of Bergen Park; Winter Park is 67 miles northwest of Denver via I-70/US 40; and Daniels Park is 21 miles south of Denver.

Denver Mountain Parks At A Glance				
Developed Parks				
Park #	Name	Acquired	Acres	County
1	Daniels	1920 & 1937	1,000.650	Douglas
2	Red Rocks & Morrison	1928 & 2001	804.190	Jefferson
3	Lookout Mountain	1916	66.110	Jefferson
4	Colorow Point	1916	0.537	Jefferson
5	Genesee	1912	2,412.720	Jefferson
6	Katherine Craig (not open to public)	1935	56.000	Jefferson
7	Starbuck	1916	11.130	Jefferson
8	Little	1917	400.340	Jefferson
9	Corwina	1916	297.820	Jefferson
10	O'Fallon	1938	860.000	Jefferson
11	Pence	1914	320.000	Jefferson
12	Deer Creek	1918	89.700	Jefferson
13	Turkey Creek	1914	61.000	Jefferson
14	Newton	1939 & 1962	431.000	Jefferson
15	Cub Creek & Dillon	1922	549.140	Jefferson
16	Bell	1915	480.000	Jefferson
17	Fillius	1914	107.674	Jefferson
18	Bergen	1915	25.431	Jefferson
19	Dedisse	1919	420.420	Jefferson
20	Echo Lake	1920	616.300	Clear Creek
21	Summit Lake	1924	161.830	Clear Creek
22	Winter Park	1939	88.900	Grand
Total	Developed Parks Acreage		9,260.892	
Conservation/Wilderness Parks				
	Forsberg		1.910	Clear Creek
	Hicks Mountain		840.000	Clear Creek
	Mt. Judge		360.000	Clear Creek
	Pence Mountain		560.000	Clear Creek
	Snyder Mountain		240.000	Clear Creek
	Bear Creek Canyon		130.000	Jefferson
	Bergen Peak		520.000	Jefferson
	Berrian Mountain		520.000	Jefferson
	Birch Hill		160.000	Jefferson
	Double Header Mountain		40.000	Jefferson
	Elephant Butte		665.100	Jefferson
	Fenders		40.000	Jefferson
	Flying "J"		80.000	Jefferson
	Hobbs Peak		40.000	Jefferson
	Legault Mountain		160.000	Jefferson
	Mt. Falcon		160.000	Jefferson
	Mt. Lindo		80.000	Jefferson
	North Turkey Creek		40.000	Jefferson
	Old Cemetery Ground		0.185	Jefferson
	Parmalee Gulch		2.880	Jefferson
	Stanley Park		80.000	Jefferson
	Strain Gulch		40.000	Jefferson
	West Jefferson School		80.000	Jefferson
	Yegge Peak		40.000	Jefferson
Total	Conservation Parks Acreage		4880.075	
TOTAL ACREAGE ALL PARKS			14,140.967	

(adapted from Denver Mountain Parks Master Plan)

SCENIC BEAUTY SPOTS

The Denver Mountain Parks

A Historic Legacy Since 1912

Today, Denver has a treasure not of gold or silver, but of beautiful preserved parks just outside its boundaries in the mountains to the west of the city. In fact, Denver owns 14,141 acres of park land in Jefferson, Clear Creek, Grand and Douglas counties, comprising 22 developed parks and 24 conservation/wilderness areas. Citizen foresight in the early 1900's preserved these pristine landscapes for the enjoyment of future generations.

Imagine Denver in 1910. It had only been in existence since 1859, so it was just over fifty years old. Population of the city was 213,381, with only 539,700 people in the entire state of Colorado. Wide open spaces were everywhere. There was hardly anyone in the mountains west of Denver. Little settlements like Morrison, Evergreen, and Bergen were only waysides on a series of rough wagon roads into the mountains. Denver's downtown streets were crowded with horses, wagons and trolleys. Newfangled automobiles were rare, and competed for space on the city's dirt roads.

How radical was it then in 1910, when John Brisben Walker Sr. proposed to the Denver Chamber of Commerce, that Denver purchase lands for parks in the mountains, and link the parks with a series of roads for automobiles? Outlandish! Crazy! Automobiles were only a passing fad. Mountain lands would always be open and empty of people and buildings. Why spend any money on Walker's crazy proposal?

Fortunately, some very important people listened to Walker, including Denver Mayor Robert Speer. Speer had attended the World's Columbian Exposition in Chicago in 1893, and was very impressed with the beautiful pavilions and malls. When he became mayor of Denver in 1904, Speer had the Chicago exposition buildings deeply impressed on his mind, and wanted to bring this "City Beautiful" to Denver. Speer wanted parks and parkways, grand buildings with columns and monuments. Speer imagined an Alameda Parkway from Denver all the way to the foot of the mountains, and a Colfax Parkway doing the same. When Walker's idea for mountain parks came along, Speer immediately warmed to the idea, and envisioned his parkways linking the city to the mountain parks.

8

Actually John Brisben Walker Sr., had been contemplating a Denver mountain parks system as early as 1880. Walker was born near Pittsburgh in 1847. He was one of the founders of Cosmopolitan Magazine, which he sold to William Randolph Hearst for the princely sum of one million dollars in 1905. In 1879 Walker visited Colorado on a tour of the west. He purchased 1,600 acres for $60,000 in north Denver for an alfalfa farm which he named "Berkeley." He sold the farm in 1888 for $325,000. With his million dollars from the sale of Cosmopolitan, he started buying up land around Red Rocks west of Denver, purchasing 4,000 acres in 1905. In 1906, Walker and his son John B. Walker Jr., spent $150,000 to create an amusement park in the Red rocks area which they named "Garden of the Titans." They immediately started staging musical performances in the acoustically perfect natural amphitheater among the rocks. In 1909, Walker and his son completed the Mount Morrison Railway Company, which consisted of a funicular railway to the top of Mount Morrison in the Garden of the Titans.

9622. The Seat of Pluto, Park of the Red Rocks and Gardens of the Titans, Mt. Morrison, Colo.

Walker had a lot at stake when he proposed the mountain parks idea to the Denver Chamber of Commerce in 1910. He wanted his Garden of the Titans to become a crown jewel in a string of parks in the mountains including Lookout Mountain, Genesee and other areas all linked by a chain of roads, so that Denver residents and visitors could view the fantastic scenery from their automobiles. A century later, Joanne Ditmer writing in the Denver Post (May 9, 2009) summed up Walker's idea beautifully: "These lands invite people of all ages and family sizes and income to have a mountain experience, to get acquainted with nature, have a picnic by a stream, take a hike, have a rare solitary meditation."

In 1911, the Denver Chamber of Commerce appointed Warwick M. Downing, a Denver lawyer, businessman and Park Commissioner, to be chairman of a committee to look into the establishment of Denver Mountain Parks. The committee looked favorably on Walker's proposal and developed a strategy to implement it. On December 7, 1911 the committee's plan was ready. It called for an amendment to the Denver city charter which would allow Denver to purchase land for park purposes outside the city limits, and asked for a mill levy of one-half percent to fund the purchases.

The campaign for the charter amendment began in earnest in 1912. This was Mayor Speer's last year in office as his popularity was in decline, and he did not seek re-election. However, he hoped his dream of parks and parkways would extend into the mountains with the passage of the charter amendment. Downing, writing in the March-April 1931 issue of Denver Municipal Facts recalled that during the campaign for the amendment "the city was placarded with maps and pictures. The most effective was the picture of a modest home, assessed at $3,000 whose owner would be taxed 50 cents a year, but whose wife and children would forever enjoy the Mountain Parks." When the election was held in May of 1912, the amendment was passed "by a substantial majority."

Genesee Mountain became the first Mountain Park in 1912, when a group of public-spirited citizens led by E.W. Merritt gave 1,200 acres on the mountain to Denver. This group saved Genesee from the ravages of a sawmill by purchasing the land from the sawmill in 1911. Thus Denver Mountain Parks were born in 1912 with the passage of the mill levy and the gift of Genesee Park. The official opening occurred on August 27, 1913 with the ceremonial opening of Genesee to visitors. Bison and elk from Yellowstone National Park were brought to graze upon the meadows of Genesee, and the bison herd that is visible from Interstate 70 today is descendant from that original Yellowstone herd. In April, 1913 the Colorado Legislature passed a bill granting Denver powers of Eminent Domain in respect to its Mountain Parks, allowing Denver to obtain park land outside its boundaries in other counties. Then in August, 1914, the U.S. Congress passed an act granting 7,047 acres of public land in the National Forests to Denver at a cost of $1.25 per acre. These two measures, along with the mill levy, allowed Denver to begin acquisition of its Mountain Parks.

Denver acted quickly, and acquired:
> 1914- Fillius Park (108 acres)
> 1914- Pence Park (320 acres
> 1914- Turkey Creek Park (61 acres)
> 1915- Bergen Park (25 acres)
> 1915- Bell Park (480 acres)

Followed by additional parks:
> 1916- Corwina Park (298 acres)
> 1916- Lookout Mountain Park (66 acres)
> 1917- Little Park (400 acres)
> 1918- Deer Creek Park (90 acres)
> 1919- Dedisse Park (420 acres)

Bison enclosure at Genesee Mountain Park.

Other parks were acquired in the 1920's including John Brisben Walker's Red Rocks, purchased in 1927 and 1928. Acquisition of all the parks was completed in 1939 with the purchase of Newton Park and Winter Park. Another 424 acres was acquired for Newton Park in 1962, and 165 more acres were purchased for Red Rocks Park in 2001, thus completing the Denver Mountain Parks system which today consists of a total of 14,141 acres.

Road Building and Circle Routes

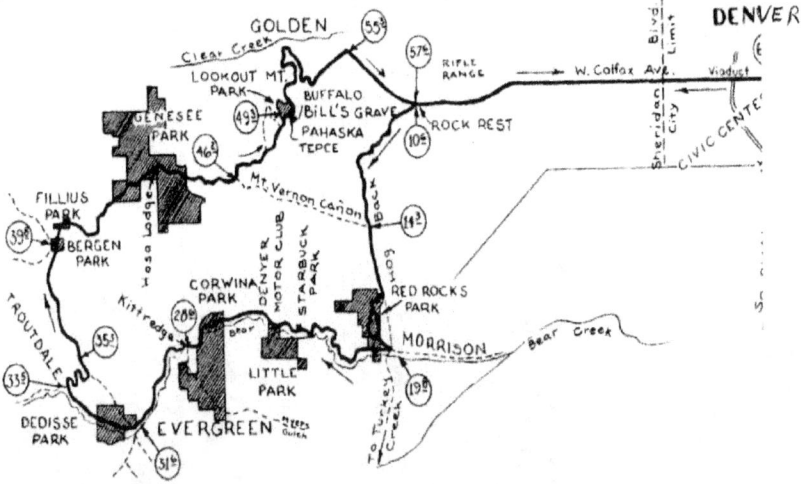

"C" Denver to Rock Rest, Hogback thru Red Rocks and Morrison, up Bear Creek to Evergreen, Troutdale Loop to Bergen Park, to Lookout, to Golden, to Denver. 68.2 M

A typical circle route of roads connecting parks- from an early Mountain Parks brochure.

Writing in the March-April, 1931 issue of Denver Municipal Facts, Warwick M. Downing (chairman of the committee to establish the Denver Mountain Parks) recalled the vision of the committee: "Our conception of a Mountain Park is a chain or series of parks somewhat in the form of a semi-circle, commencing at a point in the vicinity of Lookout Mountain, a tract in Bergen Park, a tract along Bear Creek above Evergreen, a tract in Spruce Park, a tract in Eden Park and following Turkey Creek Canon to its mouth. Each park should be connected with all the others by a well-built road, and each end of the chain should be connected with Denver by a splendid drive."

Denver hired famed landscape architect Frederick Law Olmsted Jr. in 1912 to plan the mountain park system and layout the roads. Olmsted toured the proposed mountain park areas on horseback, following trails and primitive wagon roads connecting small settlements such as Morrison, Evergreen, and Bergen Park. Olmsted eventually submitted his plan to Denver with a map showing more than 41,000 proposed acres of park land. Denver whittled this down

13

to just over 7,000 acres which were purchased in 1914. Road building began according to Olmsted's plan, and by the end of 1914 the Lariat Trail Road had been built from Golden up Lookout Mountain and west from there to Genesee saddle. Construction continued in 1915 with the road continuing on to Bergen Park, which was connected to a road coming west up Bear Creek canyon to Evergreen. By the end of 1915, the loop which began in Golden, was completed around the circle to Morrison (map page 13).

5970. Golden and Plains from Denver Mountain Parks Auto Highway.

Early postcard shows the newly completed Lariat Trail road up Lookout Mountain, with Golden in the top right distance.

With the first loop completed, Mountain Parks Commission looked to expand the road system westward. To further their goal, in 1918 they proposed to Congress establishment of a national park in the Mount Evans area. The hope was that the U.S. government would build the desired road from Bergen park to Squaw Pass and on up to Mount Evans.

The national park idea was vigorously opposed by the National Forestry Department which wanted to retain control of the Mount Evans area in the National Forest system. To placate Denver, the Forestry Department promised construction of the sought-after road. Thus the plan for a national park was abandoned, and the Forestry

Department did indeed begin road construction from Bergen Park to Squaw Pass. By August, 1919, the road was completed to Squaw Pass, and construction continued west to Echo Lake. Denver purchased Echo Lake Park (617 acres) in 1920. In 1923, building of the road from Echo Lake to Summit Lake proceeded, and Denver bought Summit Lake Park (160 acres) in 1924. Construction was eventually completed to the top of Mount Evans in 1931, and Denver had its dream road connecting its mountain parks to the top of one of the highest peaks in Colorado (14,130 feet at the parking lot; 14,264 feet at the summit).

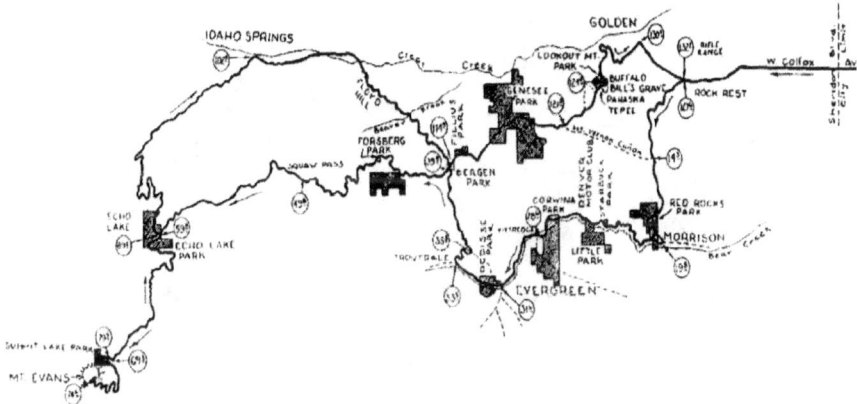

By 1931, a Mountain Parks brochure showed two completed road loops with a spur to Mt. Evans.

Another circle route promoted by Denver Mountain Parks was a drive through the southern section of the parks (see map page 16). The suggested route was from Denver south to Littleton on Santa Fe Drive, and then west on Platte Canyon Road to Deer Creek Park (acquired in 1918), continuing west to Turkey Creek Park (acquired 1914). A side trip to Conifer was suggested before going on to Turkey Creek. Today, Newton Park (acquired 1939) is just south of Conifer, so you could add that to your itinerary. North from Turkey Creek Park the road led through Indian Hills to Pence Park and then left up Bear Creek to Dedisse Park at Evergreen and on to Bergen Park, Fillius Park, Genesee, and Lookout Mountain.

15

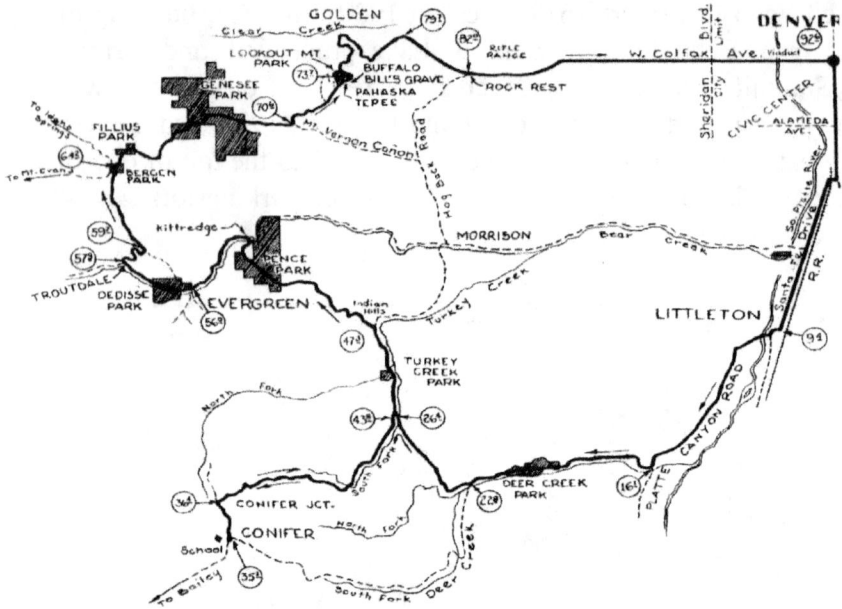

"E" Denver to Littleton, up Deer Creek to Conifer, down Turkey Creek to Indian Hills, to Bi
up to Evergreen, Loop thru Troutdale, to Bergen Park, to Lookout, to Denver.

Suggested circle route through the southern section of the Mountain Parks.

The circle routes can still be driven today, and the roads have been greatly improved since the 1930's. To drive any one of the circles requires a full day, and while the drive would certainly be scenic, there would be no time to stop in each individual park for exploration. At some of the major parks such as Red Rocks, Lookout Mountain, Genesee or the Echo Lake area, a full day could easily be spent at each park. In the next section we'll explore the 22 historic getaway trips to the individual parks.

Getaway 1- Daniels Park

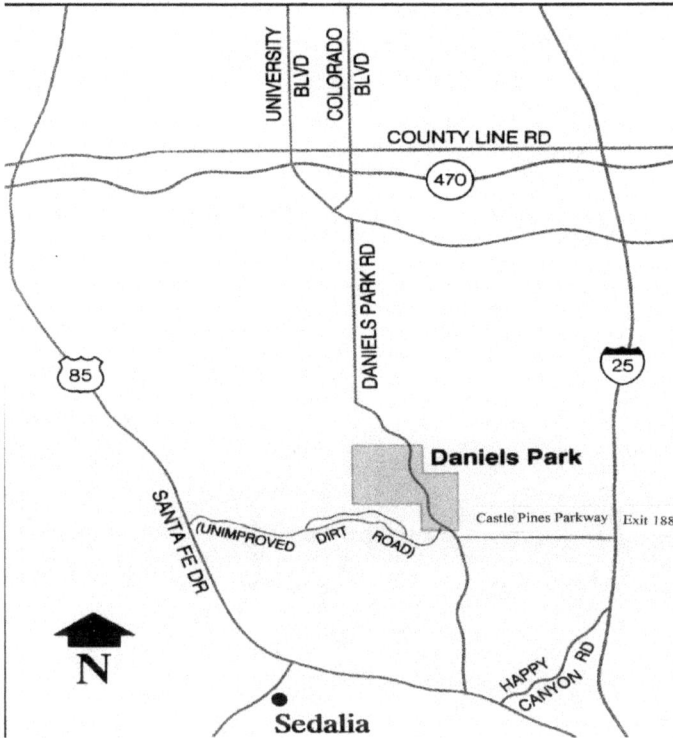

Daniels Park

Getting There-

The easiest approach to Daniels Park is to take Interstate 25 south from Denver to Exit 188 and go west on Castle Pines Parkway. Turn right at the intersection with Daniels Park Road. The western approach is from U.S. Highway 85 (Santa Fe Drive). Head southeast past Sedalia, and then turn north on Daniels Park Road. Daniels Park may also be approached heading south from Denver on either University Blvd. or Colorado Blvd. Those two streets intersect south of C-470 in Highlands Ranch and become just University Blvd. Then follow University east to Wildcat Reserve Parkway. Turn right (south). Follow Wildcat Reserve to McArthur Ranch Road and turn left. Take McArthur Ranch Road for about two blocks and then turn right on Griggs Road. Follow Griggs Road to North Daniels Park Road and turn right into the park.

The Story Behind The Park

Technically, Daniels Park is not in the mountains. It is on a high sandstone ridge about 21 miles south of Denver, with incredible western views of the entire Front Range from Pike's Peak in the south to Long's Peak in the north. It has the feel of the mountains though, with its elevation of 6,500 feet, and mixture of scrub oak and pine trees. It is the only Denver Mountain Park located in Douglas County.

Stone picnic tables along the ridge give way to sweeping views of the Rocky Mountain Front Range at Daniels Park.

The road through Daniels Park today basically follows one of the first Colorado Territorial Roads built in the 1850's linking Denver and Colorado Springs. Stagecoaches through this area were subject to ambush by robbers who hid in the many gullies nearby. In May of 1868, Kit Carson was in Daniels Park, gravely ill and hoping to return to his home in Taos, New Mexico to die there. Supposedly Carson lit a campfire to cook his noon meal, and called this his "last campfire." He died a few days later at Fort Lyons. Today, there is a stone monument marking this site at the southern end of the park.

The ranch buildings seen in Daniels Park today are the remnants of the Florence Martin Ranch. They are not open to the public and are used in maintenance of the park by Mountain Parks staff. Florence Martin was born in Sydney, Australia, in 1867, the daughter of the premier of the state of New South Wales. In 1905, she met wealthy American explorer, William Cooke Daniels who had made a fortune with the Daniels & Fisher department store in Denver. Daniels brought his fiancée, Cicely, with him to Australia. Cicely stayed with Florence while Daniels went on a sixteen month expedition to New Guinea. When Daniels returned, he married Cicely. Florence Martin then traveled with her friends to England and France, eventually returning to America when World War I broke out in 1914. Unfortunately Daniels died in 1918, and his wife soon followed him in death with the flu epidemic of 1918. Florence Martin received a large inheritance from the Daniels's. With her inheritance she purchased the land which is now Daniels Park. In 1920, Florence gave 40 acres of her land to Denver for inclusion in the Denver Mountain Parks, with the stipulation that the park be named "Daniels." Denver gladly accepted that condition. In 1937, Martin's ranch home burned down, and she decided to give Denver 960 more acres to include in Daniels Park. This large acreage allowed Daniels Park to become a buffalo preserve, and the animals were added in the late 1930's.

Buffalo (bison) roam the enclosed paddocks at Daniels Park.

Daniels Park is a gem which has preserved the pristine mountain views from the top of the rimrock. Just to the east of the park, a housing development runs right up to the buffalo fence. If Daniels Park was not here, the houses would undoubtedly go right up to the edge of the rim. Thanks to Florence Martin and her land donation, this will not happen. The bicyclist on Daniels Park Road (photo below) can enjoy the same views as the home owners on his right.

J.J.B. Benedict was a Denver architect who designed several of the rustic stone and log picnic shelters in Denver Mountain Parks, including this one at Daniels Park.

What To Do In The Park

Picnic

On a clear day, the views of the entire Front Range to the west of Daniels Park are simply incredible. Picnics along the rim are possible practically throughout the year on a sunny day, though winter excursions will require extra jackets, especially if the wind is blowing. The picnic shelter is available for group reservation by calling Denver Parks and Recreation at 720-913-0700.

Hiking

There are no defined hiking trails in Daniels Park, but short hikes along the rim and scrambling over rocks appeal to many visitors.

Biking

Cyclists can ride through the main road in the park, with connections to more bike trails to the north in Highlands Ranch, and south in Douglas County.

Bison Viewing

Enjoy safely viewing the bison behind their enclosures.

21

Getaway 2- Red Rocks Park

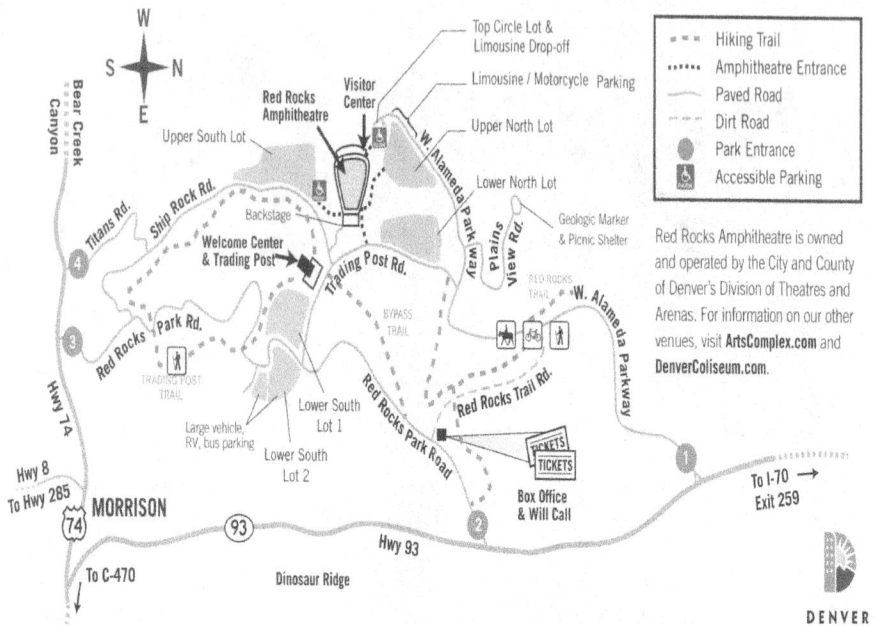

Map legend:
- Hiking Trail
- Amphitheatre Entrance
- Paved Road
- Dirt Road
- Park Entrance
- Accessible Parking

Red Rocks Amphitheatre is owned and operated by the City and County of Denver's Division of Theatres and Arenas. For information on our other venues, visit ArtsComplex.com and DenverColiseum.com.

Getting There-

Access to Red Rocks Parks is easy today, compared to the early 1900's when visitors either had to take the train out to Morrison, or take the rough wagon road fifteen miles west from Denver. From C-470 today, take the Morrison exit west on Highway 74. After passing through the quaint town of Morrison, turn right in to Red Rocks at entrance 3 (Red Rocks Park Road) or entrance 4 (Titans Road). From I-70, take exit 259 south on to Highway 93, and turn right in to Red Rocks at entrance 1 (West Alameda Parkway) or entrance 2 (Red Rocks Park Road).

361—Red Rocks Theatre, Park of the Red Rocks, Denver Mt. Parks, Colorado

The Story Behind The Park

CREATION PARK. MORRISON, COLO.

The tilting red sandstone rock formations so common in Red Rocks Park are part of the Fountain Formation, found in several places along Colorado's Front Range, from Garden of the Gods in Colorado Springs, to Roxborough State Park, Red Rocks Park, and the Flatirons in Boulder. Geologists tell us that these rocks were shed off the Ancestral Rockies as they rose up from 323 to 290 million years ago. The Red Rocks tilt about 30 degrees to the west, and they meet up against gray metamorphic rocks on the west which are 1.7 billion years old. This 1.4 billion year gap in the geologic history is known as an "unconformity."

So the Red Rocks were here when dinosaurs roamed the area about 150 million years ago. Dinosaur fossils and tracks are found in the Morrison Formation just east of Red Rocks along the Dakota Hogback. The Dinosaur Ridge Museum is located just west of C-470 at the Alameda Parkway exit, and is a worthwhile stop on any day trip to the Red Rocks area.

Human exploration of the Red Rocks area is a much more recent occurrence. Tribes of Ute, Arapaho, and Cheyenne Indians roamed the area over the past few hundred years. In fact, the Utes under chief Colorow were still in Red Rocks as late as 1877. The Utes lived in teepees and stick wickiups, much different from the Pueblo Indian style building seen at the Red Rocks Trading Post (see page 28).

Anglo settlers had to endure sporadic raids from the Utes when they settled along Bear Creek near Red Rocks in the 1860's. George Morrison, a stone mason from Montreal, homesteaded 320 acres along Bear Creek in 1864, and the growing community became the town of Morrison in 1872. George Morrison's masonry skills came in handy as he opened several rock quarries in the area which produced beautiful red sandstone rocks. To haul the rocks out from the quarries, the Denver, South Park and Pacific Railroad extended a narrow gauge line to Morrison in 1874. With the success of the stone business, the town of Morrison grew from a population of 186 in 1880 to 254 in 1890 according to the U.S. census.

George Morrison built this beautiful stone home for his family in 1873, with an addition in 1889. Today it's the Cliff House Lodge.

9611. Creation Rock, Park of the Red Rocks, and Garden of the Titans, Mt. Morrison, Colo.

25

Not only did the Denver, South Park and Pacific Railroad haul rock out of Morrison, it brought tourists from Denver eager to see the magnificent sights of nearby Red Rocks. John Brisben Walker Sr., using funds from his sale of Cosmopolitan Magazine (see page 9), purchased 4,000 acres at Red Rocks in 1905. Together with his son, John Brisben Walker Jr., they opened their "Garden of the Titans" as an amusement park on May 31, 1906. "Titans" were the most powerful creatures in Greek mythology, and the Walkers probably chose that name to indicate that their attraction was superior to the Garden of the Gods in Colorado Springs. The Walkers held concerts on Stage Rock, and in 1906 also built a 70-person observation deck atop Creation Rock (see postcard page 25). Bands performed in the summer on the deck at the top of the 400 foot high rock. It was a scramble to get up the rock with several ladders, and steps carved out of the rock.

Another unique feature of the amusement park was the funicular railway the Walkers built to the top of Mount Morrison. Construction on the "Mount Morrison Incline Railway" began in 1908, and the railway opened on September 5, 1909. Fare for the two-mile round trip ride was $1.00, which the Walkers reckoned was a bargain, because after all, a roundtrip on the Pike's Peak Cog Railway in Colorado Springs cost $5.00 at the time. The Mount Morrison Railway had two 100-seat passenger cars, one on each side of the tracks, and two cables pulled the counterbalanced cars up and down the mountain. The seats in the cars faced backwards so that as the car rose, passengers had their backs to the mountain and faced all the beautiful Red Rocks scenery below them. By 1915, the railway was shut down, and the City of Denver received only $570 for scrap iron when it sold the remains in 1929.

John Brisben Walker Sr., had always wanted his park to be included in the chain of Denver Mountain Parks. He lobbied passionately for the cause of automobile travel, and roads to connect his park with other mountain parks. However, he and the City of Denver could never see eye to eye on a selling price for his land. While the Denver Mountain Parks were established in 1912, it took until 1928 for the City and Walker to agree on a price of $50,000 for 110 acres of his Red Rocks land.

15792. Giant Rock Formation, Park of the Red Rocks, Denver Mountain Parks, Colorado

Denver in fact, had been purchasing land in the Red Rocks area since 1927, paying John Ross $25,000 for 530 acres. Thus Red Rocks Park became a Denver Mountain Park in 1928, with a total of 640 acres combining the Ross land and the Walker land. City crews began grading and constructing roads through the park in 1929, such as the one shown above which wound just below Creation Rock on the top right, and Ship Rock on the left. The eventual amphitheatre would be constructed between the two rocks from 1936-1941.

ENTERING PARK OF RED ROCKS FROM THE SOUTH

South entrance road to Red Rocks Park constructed circa 1929.

N115:–PUEBLO AT RED ROCKS, DENVER MOUNTAIN PARKS, COLORADO.

The next item of construction in the new park in 1931 was the "Pueblo" or the "Indian Concession House" as it was originally called. Designed by Denver Parks draftsman Wilbert R. Rosche, it served as visitor center, museum, and concession stand. It's architecture reflects both the Spanish mission style (front-above) and the Pueblo Indian style (side-below). Today it's called the Red Rocks Trading Post.

15791. The Pueblo Park of the Red Rocks, Denver Mountain Parks, Colorado

George Cranmer, Director of Denver Parks and Improvements Department.

The story of the creation of Red Rocks Amphitheatre really begins with George Cranmer. Cranmer was born in Denver in 1884 and attended East High School. One of his high school field trips in the early 1900's was to Red Rocks where he was extremely impressed with its beauty and acoustics. In 1928, Cranmer visited Italy including the island of Sicily, where he saw the outdoor amphitheatre constructed by the ancient Greeks at Taormina. This image stayed in his mind for years, and undoubtedly transposed itself to his memories of Red Rocks. Cranmer was Mayor Benjamin Stapleton's campaign manager for the mayor's re-election in 1935. With victory in the election, Mayor Stapleton gave Cranmer his choice of cabinet offices in Denver government. Cranmer chose to be Director of the Parks & Improvements Department. At last he had a chance to realize his dream of an amphitheatre in Red Rocks.

However, this was the depths of the Great Depression, and Denver's treasury was virtually depleted. Furthermore, Mayor Stapleton was opposed to an amphitheatre at Red Rocks, believing that the area should be kept in its natural state. Cranmer persisted though, and eventually came up with a plan to get the federal government to build the amphitheatre. To try to pull the country out of the Depression, the federal government had created several agencies such as the Works Progress Administration and the Civilian Conservation Corps to employ out-of-work young men on various projects across the country. Cranmer approached Secretary of the Interior Harold Ickes with his idea, and on May 9, 1936, Ickes agreed to use the CCC to build the amphitheatre at Red Rocks. Formed in 1933, the CCC employed male citizens between 17-25 years old, who were paid $30/month, and enlisted for 6-month periods of time, up to a maximum of two years.

The natural setting in the 1930's before amphitheatre construction began.

The CCC had already established a camp in Morrison on the south banks of Bear Creek in 1935, so when the assignment came to build the Red Rocks amphitheatre, they didn't have far to travel. The workers first camped out in tents while they built barracks to live in. The camp at Morrison housed 215 workers. It took from 1936-1941 for the CCC workers to complete work on Red Rocks Amphitheatre. The site for the amphitheatre was filled with tons of boulders which had to be cleared. Cranmer arranged for the CCC to do all of the blasting in one day, and it chanced to be on a day when Mayor Stapleton (who was still not pleased with disturbing the natural setting) happened to be out of town. After blasting, pulverized rock remnants were then scraped downhill to fill out the natural bowl of the amphitheatre.

Morrison CCC barracks building in center now serves as Denver Mountain Parks headquarters.

Red Rocks Amphitheatre was designed by famed Denver architect Burnham Hoyt. Hoyt's plan was to leave as much of the natural setting as possible, and make the amphitheatre blend in with the natural surroundings. Once Hoyt's plan was approved by the National Park Service (a division of Harold Ickes' Department of the Interior), the CCC began construction of the amphitheatre in 1936. After grading the seating space, the CCC workers began building the rows of seats. The project was estimated to take two years, but it took five. The grand opening of the amphitheatre was on June 15, 1941.

This statue of a CCC worker was placed at the top of the amphitheatre near the new Visitor Center in 2004, in honor of the builders of the Red Rocks amphitheatre.

Celebration of the new amphitheatre was rudely interrupted later in 1941, when the Japanese bombed Pearl Harbor, plunging America into World War II. Activity virtually ceased at the amphitheatre until after the war was over. One of the first post-war events was the first Easter sunrise service on April 6, 1947. Over the next 50 years, dozens of concerts were held each year, featuring just about every type of music imaginable, from rock n' roll, to country, to blues, to classical. Today, Red Rocks averages about 50 events a year in a 150 day season.

After 50 years, Red Rocks Amphitheatre began showing definite signs of wear and tear by the mid 1990's. Restroom facilities were deplorable, vandals had defaced the juniper planter boxes and the seating benches, parking and roads needed repair, trails were deteriorated, signage inadequate. Red Rocks needed a facelift from top to bottom. Working from a 1995 Red Rocks Master Plan, Mayor Wellington Webb proposed $22 million worth of improvements for the park in 1999. The plan caused great controversy because of the scope of the changes to the historic amphitheatre. The juniper trees were to be removed to make room for box seating. 1,400 seats were to be added by narrowing the seat space in the rows and adding seating risers on the top. Additional restrooms and concessions were to be placed on the south slope- an area that had always been an open, grassy area.

All these changes were too much for historic preservationists to accept, so after much debate, a new plan was announced in September, 2001, which dropped all the controversial changes, and added a new Visitor Center to the top of the amphitheatre. The $15 million Visitor Center would be placed out of sight underground, beneath the top seating row of the amphitheatre. This plan actually fit in with original architect Burnham Hoyt's plan to have an "agora" or marketplace at the top of the amphitheatre, which due to lack of funding had been eliminated in 1941. The City also purchased 193 acres of land adjacent to the park for $2 million, to protect the park from further encroachment by suburban homes. So construction began on the Visitor Center, where tons of dirt and rock were scooped out from behind the top seating rows.

Excavation and construction of the new Visitor Center began in 2002.

Steel I-beams were placed in concrete footers, and then a flat concrete surface poured on top of the steel. Red flagstone pavers were laid on top of the concrete, to create a large open "agora" at the top of the amphitheater. A round flagstone tower was built to encase an elevator to take visitors from the top down to the Visitor Center below. The Visitor Center is a beautiful showpiece attraction today, complete with restrooms, souvenir concessions, and full-service restaurant. It opened with a Grand Opening celebration on May 15, 2003.

Visitor Center elevator tower with Creation Rock in the background.

What To Do In The Park

Round tower marks elevator entrance to Visitor Center which is below the paved area in the foreground. Mount Morrison is in the background.

Visitor Center & Amphitheatre

Perhaps the best place to begin your visit to Red Rocks is the Visitor Center, completed in 2003. However, don't look for the Visitor Center at one of the entrances to the park. The Visitor Center is located high at the very top of the amphitheatre. The easiest way to reach the Visitor Center is to drive W. Alameda Parkway (entrance #1- see map page 22) all the way to the Top Circle Lot. Most of the parking spaces there are reserved for handicapped parking, but you may get lucky and find a place to park. If the lot is full, parking is available on the roadside leading to the lot, or at the Upper North Lot. If you have elderly guests with you, you may want to drop them off at the Top Circle Lot, and then go park the car. If you have young, ambitious guests with you, you could park at the Lower North Lot or the Upper South Lot, and then hike up the 69 rows of seats in the amphitheatre to the top.

The Top Circle Lot offers handicap-accessible passenger drop-off for the short walk to the Visitor Center.

The Visitor Center has the latest maps and brochures to guide you through your visit. It also has rest rooms, snack bar, souvenirs, historic interpretive displays including Performers Hall of Fame, and a full-service restaurant at the Ship Rock Grille. The view at the top entrance to the Visitor Center is truly amazing. You gaze down at the 9,450 seat amphitheatre with its covered stage and Stage Rock forming the backdrop behind.

The view from the stage up the amphitheatre is just about as spectacular as the view from the top down. Ship Rock is on the left and Creation Rock is on the right. The open box in the center is the film projection area. When there is not a concert in the park, visitors are free to go on the stage to sing or dance, pretending to be a rock star.

A favorite activity for fitness buffs is running straight up the rows of stairs or seats from the bottom to the top, while others jog lengthwise across the rows from one end to the other all the way to the top. Elevation at the top is 6,400 feet, so visitors from lower elevations need to take care when climbing the stairs to the top. Shortness of breath and dizziness are common symptoms, and may become severe. Allow plenty of time for walking up the stairs, and carry a bottle of water to keep yourself hydrated.

There are two other entrances to the amphitheatre in addition to the Visitor Center/Plaza entrance. Parking in the Lower North Lot (see map page 22) will lead you up to the East Stairs Entrance. This is quite a long climb, up a fairly steep staircase. Parking in the Upper South Lot will lead you to the South Ramp Entrance. There are no stairs on this ramp, so wheelchairs may ascend the ramp, though it too is a fairly steep grade. Additional parking is available even further below the amphitheatre at the Lower South Lots, but that will involve a long uphill hike past the Trading Post to the South Ramp Entrance.

East Stairs Entrance to the amphitheatre from the Lower North Lot, involves a lot of stair climbing.

South Ramp Entrance to the amphitheatre from the Upper South Lot allows wheelchair access up the ramp.

Concerts and Events

Approximately 50 concerts and events are held in the amphitheatre from Easter through early October. Access to the parking lots is restricted to ticket holders several hours before the events begin. If you are going to Red Rocks Park to hike, bike, or climb the amphitheatre stairs, be sure to check the website (www.redrocksonline.com) to see if there is an event scheduled that day.

Biking

Bicycling is restricted to the roads in the park and the Red Rocks Trail. Bikes are not allowed on the Trading Post Trail. Roads have heavy traffic, and cyclists should take all necessary precautions.

Picnics

Picnics are allowed throughout the park. Be sure to park only in designated parking spaces and not on the roads. There is a picnic shelter at the end of Plains View Road which can be accessed from W. Alameda Parkway.

Hiking/Climbing

The Trading Post Trail is a 1.4 mile loop trail which starts at the Red Rocks Trading Post. Take W. Alameda Parkway to Trading Post Road, and park in the lot at the Trading Post. The trail winds through beautiful red rock formations, is not overly strenuous, and can be completed in an hour or so. For more hiking opportunities you will find the Red Rocks Trailhead about halfway up the W. Alameda Parkway entrance road. You can hike the Red Rocks Trail south into the Park, or north to Matthews/Winters Open Space Park. Rock climbing is prohibited in the park, and violators face significant fines.

Trading Post Trail begins at Trading Post parking lot.

Scenic Drives

See the map on page 22. There are two scenic loop drives: 1) Red Rocks Park Road to Trading Post Road to Ship Rock Road; and 2) Highway 93 to Red Rocks Park Road to Trading Post Road to W. Alameda Parkway. The two loops can be combined into a longer figure-eight drive.

Getaway 3- Lookout Mountain Park

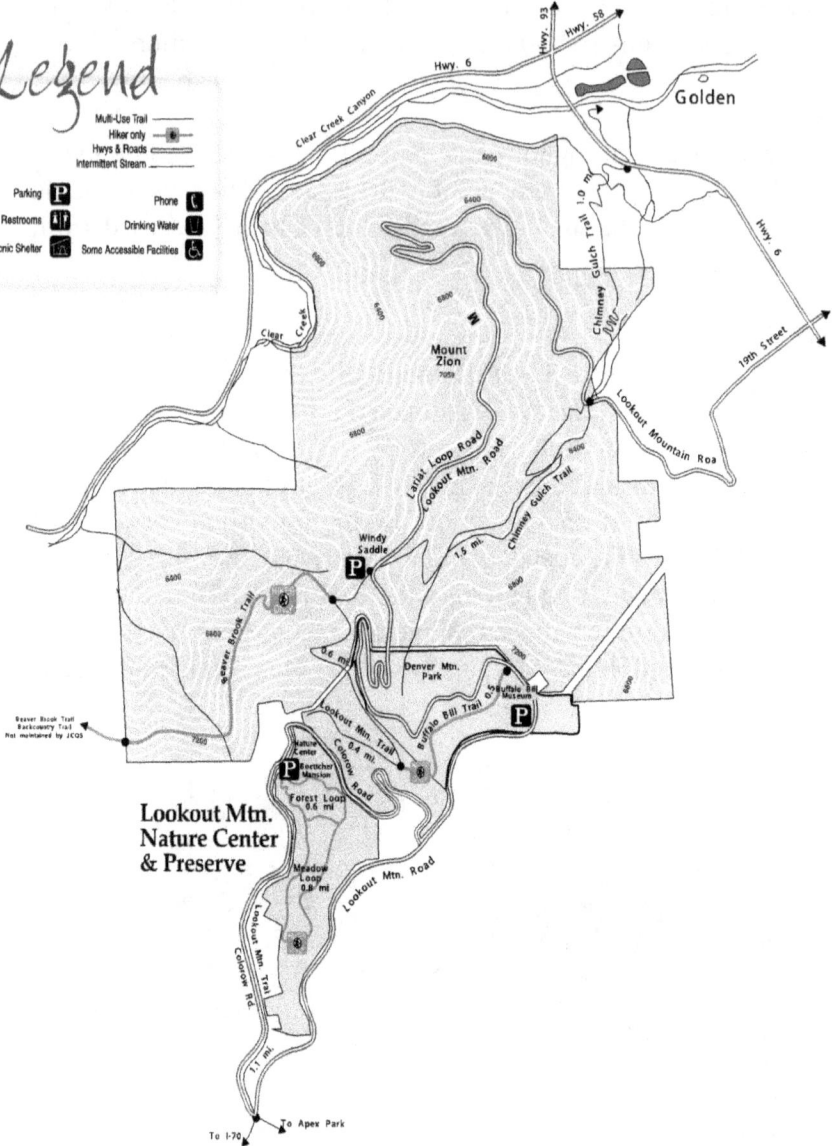

Getting There-

From Highway 6 in Golden, turn west on 19th Street, and follow Lookout Mountain Road (the Lariat Trail) 4.6 miles to the Buffalo Bill Museum and Grave at the top of the mountain (right "P" on the map above.)

The Story Behind The Park

When Denver acquired 66 acres for a mountain park on Lookout Mountain in 1916, the area had already been used as a park for a few years. The stone picnic shelter (center background in photo above) was designed by architects W.E. and A.A. Fischer and completed in 1913. In 1912, Rees Vidler, a British real estate developer who owned most of the top of Lookout Mountain, built a funicular railway from Golden to the top. Vidler dreamed of a resort community on top with a hotel, lake, and golf course. To court buyers for lots in his resort, he brought them up his railway to admire the scenic view. Unfortunately for Vidler, he was not able to attract many buyers, and he gave up his plan just a few years later. Fortunately though, he did give 58 acres on the top of the mountain to Denver, and this became the basis for Lookout Mountain Park in the Denver Mountain Parks system.

5987. Funicular Railroad to Top of Lookout Mountain.
DENVER MOUNTAIN PARKS

LOOKOUT MOUNTAIN PARK
FUNICULAR

To attract a lot more visitors to Lookout Mountain than the funicular railway could handle, it was necessary to build a road which would bring thousands of automobiles to the top. "Cement" Bill Williams of Golden was just the visionary to do so. Williams wanted Golden to be the gateway to Denver Mountain Parks, so Golden would benefit from tourist spending also. In order to get his vision going, Williams used his own savings to build a two-foot wide trail up Lookout Mountain as far as Windy Point in 1911. Williams then gained funding from Denver, Jefferson County, and the state of Colorado, and was able to start construction on the road to the top. Other donations included $1,000 from Adolph Coors, and Charles Boettcher donated materials from his Ideal Cement Company. By the end of 1914, the road had been extended from the top of Lookout Mountain all the way out to Genesee saddle, according to Frederick Law Olmsted's original design for Mountain Park roads.

CONTINENTAL DIVIDE, FROM DENVER MOUNTAIN PARKS.

The Lariat Trail ascending to Windy Point, the last curve in the middle of the photo.

In 1917, these two stone pillars were erected marking the entrance to the Lariat Trail and Denver Mountain Parks on 19th Street in Golden. They were constructed by Finlay L. MacFarland, a Denver civic booster and mountain park devotee. Born in Missouri in 1862, MacFarland was financially successful in Colorado with a wholesale produce business in Denver from 1884-1893, and an asphalt street paving business from 1903-1912. He also was owner and president of the MacFarland Auto Company until 1925, so promoting this road was good for his business interests. On the left pillar there is a plaque denoting the "Entrance to Denver's Mountain Parks" and on the right pillar there is a plaque commemorating MacFarland's donation.

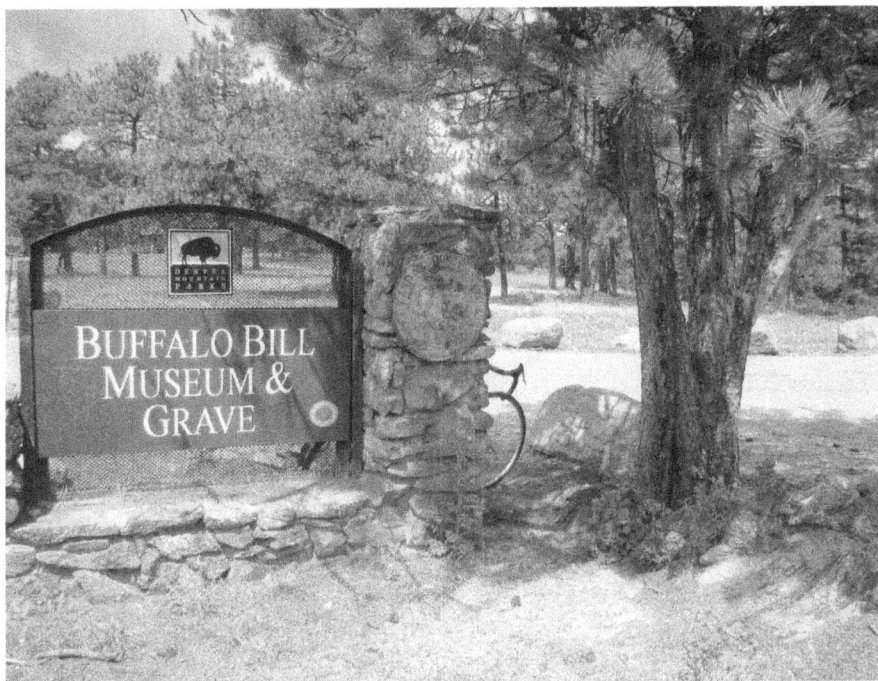

By his own request, wild west frontiersman William "Buffalo Bill" Cody was buried at the high point of Lookout Mountain Park in 1917. Cody was born in LeClaire, Iowa in 1846, but grew up in Kansas before leaving home at age 11 to herd cattle and work as a driver on a wagon train. He was a Pony Express rider in 1860, and served in the 7th Kansas Volunteer Cavalry in the Civil War from 1864-1865. In 1867 he was hired by the Kansas Pacific Railroad to provide meat for the railroad workers, and over the next 17 months killed approximately 4,280 buffalo, earning his nickname of "Buffalo Bill." After that, he was a contract scout for the U.S. Army and fought in nine different battles with the Indians from 1868-1869. From 1873-1878 Cody acted in dramas about his life on theater stages from New York to Chicago to St. Louis. Then he developed his own show-Buffalo Bill's Wild West Show, complete with buffalo, horses, sharpshooters, cowboys, and Indians. This show traveled around the USA from 1879-1886, and then moved on to Europe from 1887-1892. The show finally ended up in Denver from roughly 1910-1912, where it ran into financial difficulties and was sold. Buffalo Bill returned to Denver in 1916, gradually declining in health. He told his wife and family that he wanted to be buried on Lookout Mountain overlooking Denver. He died on January 10, 1917, and was buried at the top of Lookout Mountain on June 3, 1917. His body was kept at Olinger's Mortuary in Denver until the burial. According to newspaper reports, 20,000 people attended the burial, making for a massive traffic jam on the Lariat Trail. His wife Louisa died on October 20, 1921, and she was buried next to her husband on Lookout Mountain.

15666. Buffalo Bill Museum and Grave, Lookout Mt., Colo.

After Buffalo Bill's death, his stepson Johnny Baker proposed a building to the City of Denver on Lookout Mountain which would hold the artifacts from Cody's career as a buffalo hunter, army scout, and wild west showman. He wrote: "I have a collection which would be of great interest to the visitors to Lookout Mountain, and if it is possible to get a location adjacent to his tomb, I would erect a building to conform to the architecture of the Mountain Parks scheme," (Friesen, Buffalo Bill: Scout, Showman, Visionary, p. 151). Denver accepted Baker's proposal, and the mountain chalet-style building shown in the postcard above was the result. Baker named the building "Pahaska Tepee" after Buffalo Bill's hunting lodge near Yellowstone National Park. The museum opened on Memorial Day, 1921. Baker also operated a gift shop and restaurant in the building to

48

pay for expenses. When Baker died in 1931, his wife Olive continued to operate the museum until her death in 1956. At that time, per prior agreement, ownership of the building reverted to the City of Denver. Denver continued operating the museum in Pahaska Tepee until 1979, when the museum was moved into a new building just down the hill. Pahaska Tepee became entirely a gift shop and restaurant operated by a concessionaire, while the City of Denver continued to operate the museum- an arrangement which stands to the present day.

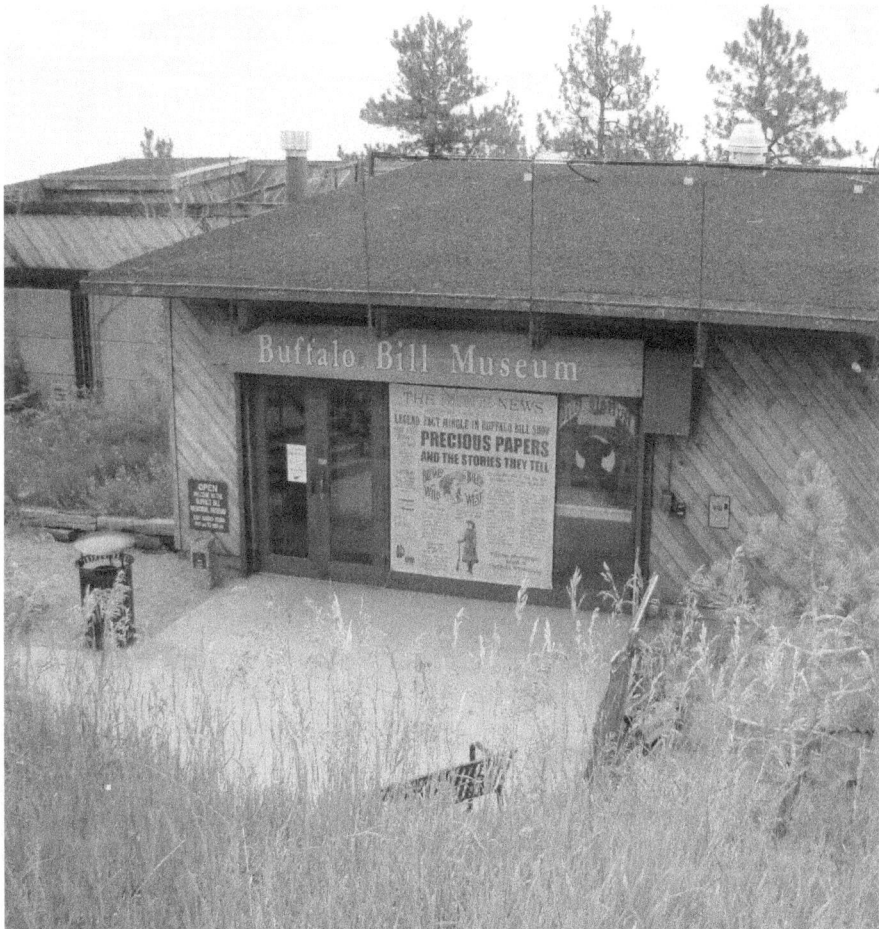

The Buffalo Bill Museum was moved from Pahaska Tepee to this building which was constructed next door in 1979.

What To Do In The Park

GOLDEN AND THE LARIAT TRAIL CLIMBING LOOKOUT MOUNTAIN FROM CASTLE ROCK

In this old postcard view, Lookout Mountain is actually to the far left, and Mt. Zion is in the middle with an "M" on it. The "M" consists of white-washed stones first placed there by students of Golden's Colorado School of Mines in 1908.

Scenic Drive

With the historical significance of the Lariat Trail and the fantastic views from the road, your trip to Lookout Mountain Park really should begin in Golden (see map page 42). You can however, get to Lookout Mountain Park from I-70 west, Exit 256. Driving the Lariat Trail is a thrill, both going up and coming down from Lookout Mountain. Sometimes the road is closed for bicycle or running races, so the I-70 route is then a viable alternative.

Biking

The 4.6 mile Lariat Trail is the way to go for bicyclists also. The road is very curvy and steep, and should be attempted by experienced cyclists only.

50

Paragliding/Hang Gliding

The launch spot for gliders is just above the "M" on Mt. Zion, so watch for them sailing loftily above you while driving the Lariat Trail.

Picnics

The picnic shelter in Lookout Mountain Park, built in 1913, still hosts family gatherings today. Call Denver Parks at 720-913-0700 for reservations. There are also picnic tables scattered throughout the park, and my favorite picnic spot is sitting on the rocks at the north end of the Buffalo Bill Museum parking lot observing the view below.

Hiking

Two short one-mile trails originate in Lookout Mountain Park at the Buffalo Bill Museum parking lot. One trail goes down to Windy Saddle on the Lariat Trail. The other trail goes west to Colorow Point Park and the Lookout Mountain Nature Center and Preserve.

Buffalo Bill Museum and Grave

Buffalo Bill's grave is accessed by a short paved trail from the parking lot to the knoll on top of Lookout Mountain. The museum is just north of Pahaska Tepee and is well worth the small entry fee. Exhibits include posters from Buffalo Bill's Wild West Show and many personal artifacts.

Pahaska Tepee Gift Shop

This building originally housed the museum, but now has an incredible collection of gifts and souvenirs. Be sure to stop in the cafe for bison burgers, bison chili, homemade fudge, and the best root beer floats on Lookout Mountain.

Getaway 4- Colorow Point Park

Getting There-
See the map on page 42. From Lookout Mountain Park, keep traveling west on Lookout Mountain Road and turn right on Colorow Road. This will take you to Lookout Mountain Nature Center & Preserve. Directly north of the Preserve, there is a small parking area where a short trail leads down to Colorow Point Park. This is the smallest Denver Mountain park, 1/2 acre in size, but the views from the point are spectacular, with Clear Creek Canyon below.

15304. Clear Creek Canyon from Colorow Point

The Story Behind The Park

Denver acquired Colorow Point in 1916. Legend has it that Ute Chief Colorow, who with his band roamed the Red Rocks Park area until 1877, leapt from this point to his death 2,000 feet below in Clear Creek Canyon rather than surrender to his pursuers.

Just to the south of Colorow Point is the Lookout Mountain Nature Center and Preserve, dedicated on November 7, 1997, commemorating 25 years since the establishment of the Jefferson County Open Space Fund in 1972. Inside of the Preserve is the

52

Boettcher Mansion, built by successful businessman Charles Boettcher, as his summer home in 1917. Born in Germany in 1852, Boettcher emigrated to the USA in 1869, and made a fortune in several businesses in Colorado including hardware, silver mines in Leadville, sugar beet processing plants, meatpacking plants, and cement. Boettcher became one of Denver's greatest philanthropists, establishing the Boettcher Foundation in 1937 to provide for a number of charitable activities. Boettcher Concert Hall in Denver is named after him.

What To Do In The Park

Picnic

Walk down to Colorow Point and enjoy a picnic on the rocks with incredible views of Clear Creek Canyon below. Be extremely cautious near the sheer cliff drop-offs. Picnics can also be enjoyed anywhere on the grounds of the Lookout Mountain Nature Center and Preserve.

Hiking

Take the one mile trail from Colorow Point east to Lookout Mountain Park and the Buffalo Bill Museum. There are also several short loop trails to hike within the Lookout Mountain Nature Center and Preserve.

Biking

Colorow Road and Lookout Mountain Road form a loop around the Lookout Mountain Nature Center and Preserve. With a fairly level surface compared to the Lariat Trail, this is a popular cycling route, however vehicular traffic is heavy.

Boettcher Mansion

Located on the grounds of the Lookout Mountain Nature Center and Preserve, the mansion is a lovely building worth a stroll around on the paved walks through gardens and trees. The Mansion is open to the public during brief periods- call 720-497-7630 for hours.

Lookout Mountain Nature Center

This modern mountain chalet style building (photo below) has excellent displays of wildlife and plants found in the local area. Admission is free. Restrooms are available in the building.

Getaway 5- Genesee Park and Katherine Craig Park

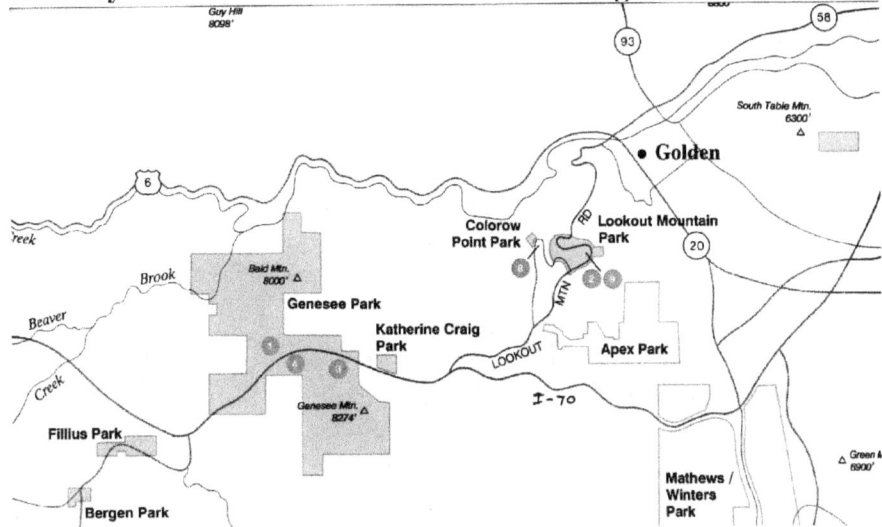

Getting There-

Simply take Interstate 70 west from Denver to Exit 254- southbound will take you into the park, and northbound will take you to an overlook of the bison herd. You can also travel west on I-70 to Exit 253- southbound will take you to Chief Hosa Lodge and Campground and on into the park. Northbound will take you to the ropes course, the Braille Trail, and the Beaver Brook Trailhead (see the map on page 56).

I-70 cuts through the heart of Genesee Park with north Genesee on the right and south Genesee on the left.

55

Genesee Mountain Park
Facilities Map

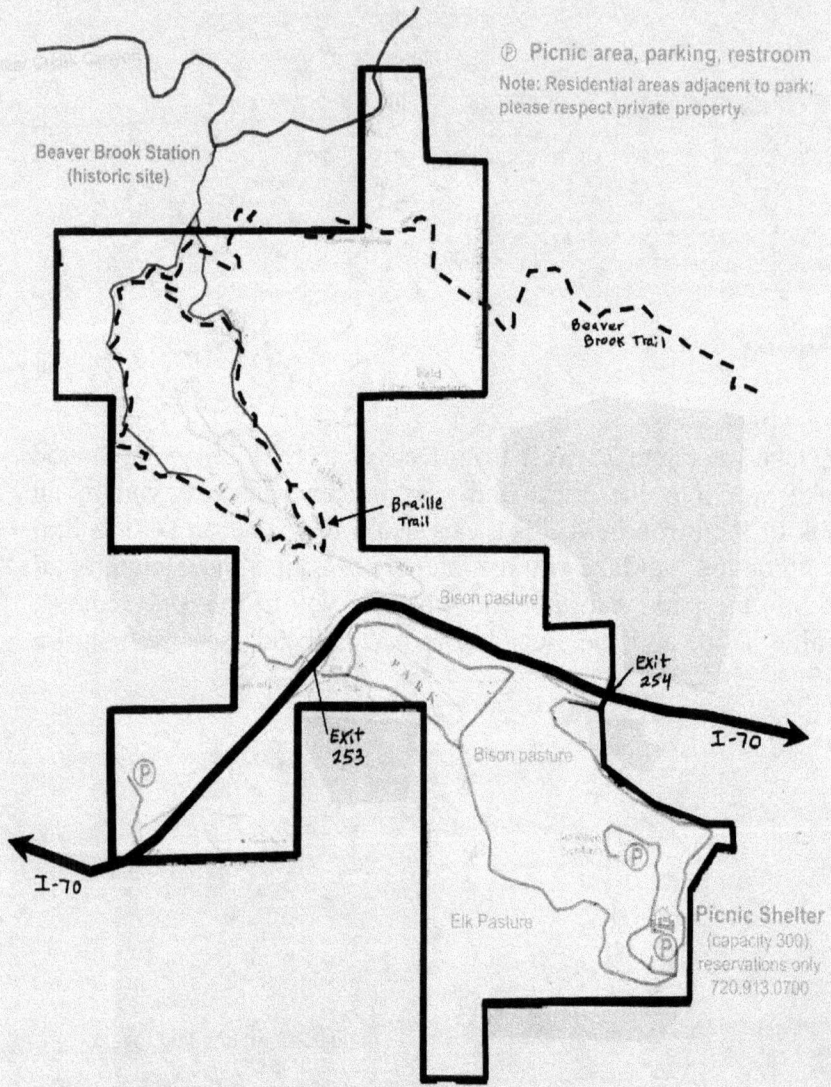

Ⓟ Picnic area, parking, restroom
Note: Residential areas adjacent to park; please respect private property.

Beaver Brook Station
(historic site)

Beaver Brook Trail

Braille Trail

Bison pasture

Exit 254

Exit 253

I-70

I-70

Bison pasture

Elk Pasture

Picnic Shelter
(capacity 300);
reservations only
720.913.0700

The Story Behind The Park

Genesee Park, Denver's first (1912) and largest (2,413 acres) Mountain Park is a gentle, sublime park, which does not immediately overwhelm the visitor in the way that Red Rocks or Lookout Mountain does. Genesee is rolling, forested hills and mountain pastures where bison graze, yet the top of the mountain (8,284 feet) offers views as spectacular as those of the other parks. Thanks to the generosity of a group of public-spirited citizens led by E.W. Merritt, Genesee was saved from the ravages of a sawmill when the group purchased 1,200 acres on the mountain in 1911. In 1912, with the passage of the mill levy for Mountain Parks in Denver, the group gave the Genesee land to Denver for its first Mountain Park. Bison and elk were brought in from Yellowstone to graze on Genesee's pastures, and the park officially opened for visitors with a celebration on August 27, 1913.

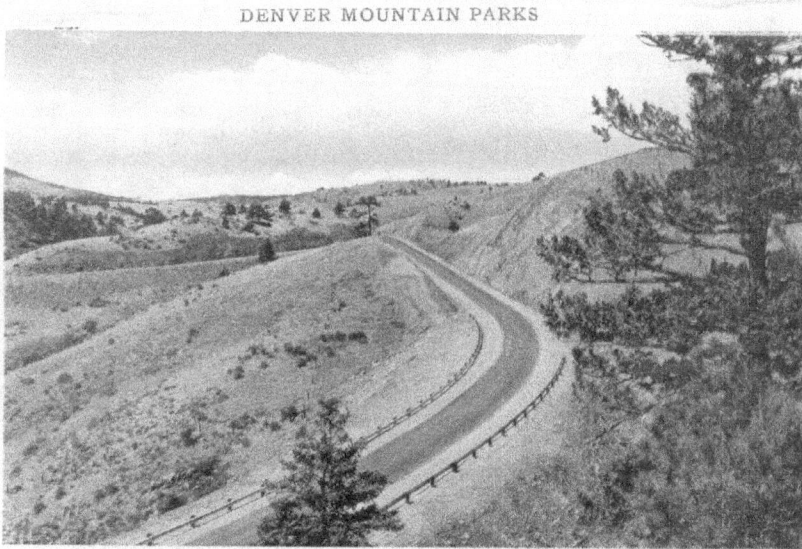

DENVER MOUNTAIN PARKS

15819. Mount Vernon Canyon, Denver Mountain Parks, Colorado

The road up Mount Vernon Canyon to Genesee Park, was not completed until 1937 by workers of the Depression-era Works Progress Administration. Prior to that time, automobile travelers had to travel up the Lariat Trail on Lookout Mountain and then follow the

Frederick Law Olmsted-designed Lookout Mountain Road out to Genesee Park. The new 1937 highway, U.S. 40, bisected Genesee Park into nearly equal sized north and south sections. This created a problem for the bison herd which had previously grazed on both sides. A tunnel was constructed under U.S. 40 to allow the bison to go from one pasture to the other. Now six lanes wide, Interstate Highway 70, completed in 1972, took even more bison pasture for concrete, and the tunnel was extended in length under the six lanes.

The Story Behind The Park- North Side

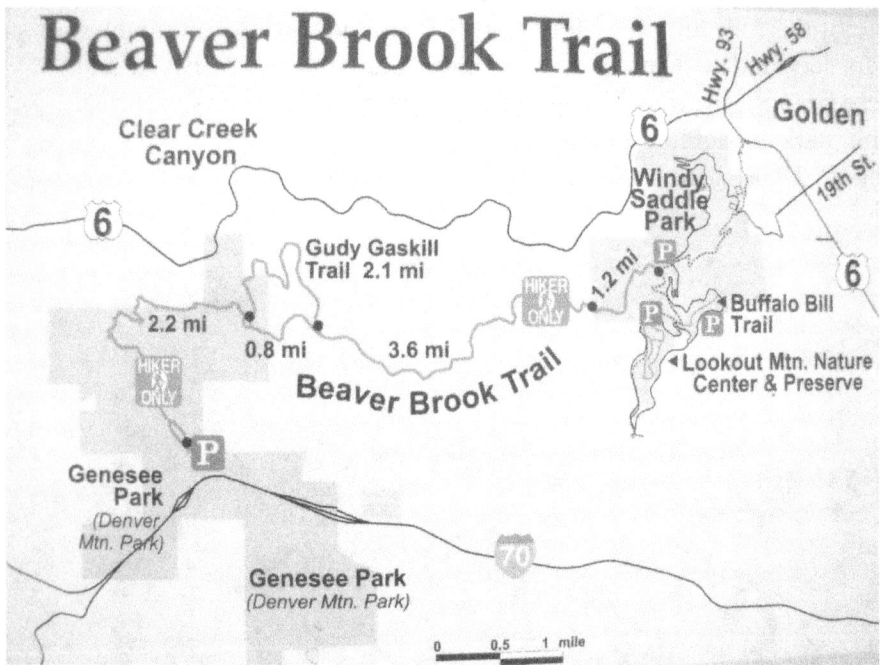

The Colorado Mountain Club, formed in Denver in 1912, persuaded the City of Denver to build the Beaver Brook Trail as an important access way to Genesee Park. The trail was constructed from 1917-1918. In the 1920's Denver acquired legal easement access to protect the trail's future. Encroachment from nearby landowners has constantly threatened the trail. Today, large homes just beyond the trail mar the wilderness hiking experience. Fortunately, in 1986, the Clear Creek Land Conservancy was established to protect the trail and Clear Creek Canyon from further development.

58

Civilian Conservation Corps barracks in Katherine Craig Park.

Workers of the 1930's era Civilian Conservation Corps who built the Genesee picnic shelter (page 61) were housed in barracks built in Katherine Craig Park just northeast of Genesee Park. The Craig family from Virginia settled in this area in 1870, and daughter Katherine grew up here. Eventually, she became Superintendent of Jefferson County Public Schools, and at three different times from 1905 - 1930 she was elected to the position of State Superintendent of Public Instruction. In 1935, she gave 56 acres of her land to Denver Mountain Parks "for the education of youth." To fulfill her bequest, Mountain Parks has leased Katherine Craig Park to the Mile High Council of Girl Scouts for use as a camp known as Camp Genesee. In addition to the CCC buildings, the camp has a ball field with backstop, picnic shelter and tables. The park is not open to the public.

The Story Behind The Park- South Side

Genesee Park was originally home to roving bands of Arapaho Indians. "Genesee" is supposedly a Native American name meaning "shining valley." Chief Little Raven, an Arapaho chief, was also known as Chief Hosa which according to David Peri (former concessionaire at Chief Hosa Lodge) means "one who works for peace," (Westword, 4/20/2006). "Chief Hosa declared Genesee a sacred ground where no blood should ever be spilled."

32 CHIEF HOSA LODGE ON LOOKOUT MOUNTAIN. DENVER MOUNTAIN PARKS. COLORADO

More accurately, the postcard caption should have read "Chief Hosa Lodge on Lookout Mountain Road..." The lodge is in Genesee Park.

Chief Hosa Lodge was designed by Denver architect Jules Jacques Benoit Benedict, and was completed in 1918. Just to the west of the lodge, a public campground opened in 1913, as America's "first Motor-Camping area." Motorists could drive up the Lariat Trail and on out Lookout Mountain Road to Genesee for a night of camping under the stars. The campground and lodge were also popular destinations for visitors who traveled by trolley to Golden, and then boarded the Colorado Central Railroad for the ride up Clear Creek Canyon to Beaver Brook Station. From there, they hiked up the Beaver Brook Trail to Chief Hosa Lodge and campground, spending the night there, and returning to Golden and Denver the next day.

On the scenic drive through the south side of Genesee Park (see page 62) you will come across a two-story white frame house built by the Patrick family in 1860 as a toll station to collect tolls from wagons and travelers heading up Mount Vernon Canyon. Today, it's home for the bison caretaker of the Genesee Park herd.

The large stone picnic shelter on the south side of Genesee Park was built by the Civilian Conservation Corps in 1939.

What To Do In The Park- North Side

Bison Viewing
Take I-70 Exit 254 and drive north a block to the parking area on the left side of the road. The Genesee Park bison herd can often be seen here.

Ropes Course
Take I-70 Exit 253 and drive north and then turn right on Stapleton Drive to the parking area. The ropes course is open to organized educational groups only. Call 720-865-0680 for information.

Hiking
Take I-70 Exit 253 and drive north and then turn right on Stapleton Drive to the parking area. The Braille Trail is a .6 mile loop with signs in Braille, and a waist-high guide wire. The Beaver Brook Trail also begins here. It's an exciting 7.8 mile hike (see map page 58) above Clear Creek Canyon which will take you back to Windy Saddle on Lookout Mountain. This trail is truly one of the great wilderness experiences in the Denver metro area. Take two cars and park one at each end of the trail to avoid doubling back on the trail.

What To Do In The Park- South Side
Scenic Drive
To make a circle drive tour of Genesee Park (see map page 56) it's easiest to go west on I-70 to Exit 253 and follow the roads through the park back east to Exit 254. South from Exit 253 you will find Chief Hosa campground on the right, and Chief Hosa Lodge on the left. Continue on up the road from Chief Hosa and turn left at the fork in the road. Travel down the hill to view the historic Patrick House. Then turn around from there and head back up the hill past the Genesee Park entrance sign. Often you will see bison in the pasture on the left. Farther up the hill on the right the high fencing encloses the elk herd. Continuing on up the hill, take the next left turn to go to the picnic shelter. From the picnic shelter drive on up the road to the summit of Genesee Mountain marked by the flagpole at 8,284 feet. Park just below the flagpole, and take the short walk to the top. Here there are excellent views of Mount Evans to the southwest, and front range peaks to the north and west. When you've finished viewing, drive back down to the picnic shelter, and just beyond it, turn left to take the curving road back down to Interstate 70 at Exit 254.

Chief Hosa Lodge

The lodge is a great place for banquets, weddings, and other parties. Call 720-913-0766 for information and reservations.

Chief Hosa Campground

This campground is the only place where camping is allowed in Denver Mountain Parks. It accommodates RV's and tents and is open from May 1 through the third week of September. Call 303-526-1324 for reservations.

Picnic

The stone picnic shelter house can be reserved by calling720-913-0700. The parking area is quite large and serves many picnic tables throughout the area, all of which are open to the public. The picnic area also has a softball field, volleyball area, and horseshoe pits.

Biking

Cycling is great on the scenic drive described on page 62.

Hiking

Short trails exist from the flagpole on top to the picnic areas.

Getaway 6- Morrison Park and Bear Creek Canyon Park

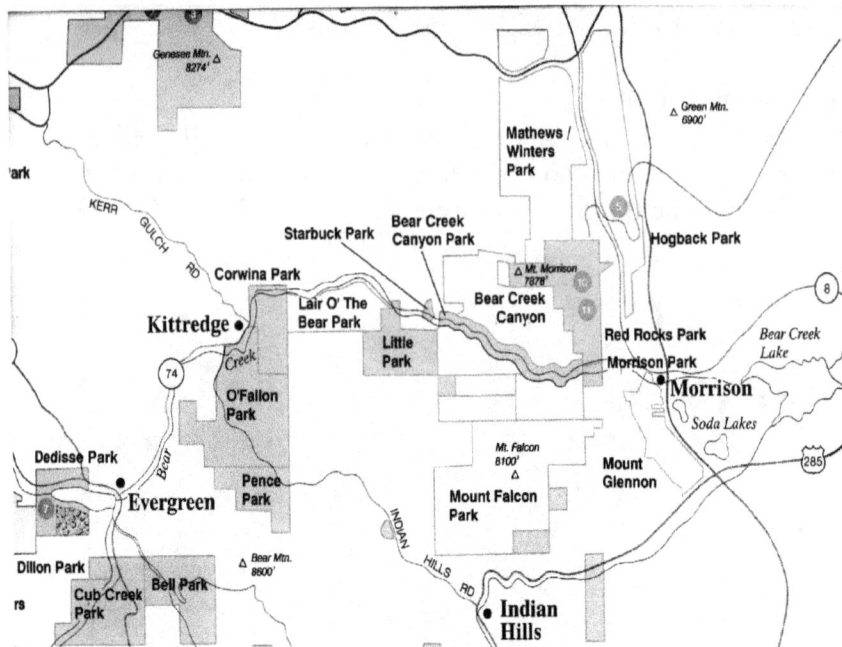

Getting There-

The easiest way to get to the entire chain of Bear Creek Parks is to travel on Highway C-470 to the Morrison Exit and then head west on Highway 74. In Morrison turn left from Highway 74 to southbound Highway 8. Then take the second right turn into Morrison Park. For Bear Creek Canyon Park, return to Highway 74 and proceed west. Morrison can also be reached by traveling west on Interstate 70, exiting at the Morrison Exit southbound on County Road 93. Then turn right (west) on Highway 74. Finally, Morrison can be approached from westbound Highway 285. Turn north on Highway 8 and drive past the Fort Restaurant to Morrison Park, which will be a left turn just before reaching Highway 74.

The Story Behind The Parks

305. BEAR CREEK ENTRANCE TO DENVER MOUNTAIN PARKS.

DENVER MOUNTAIN PARKS, COLORADO.

Like the Lariat Trail, the Bear Creek entrance to the Mountain Parks had stone pillars. Unlike the Lariat Trail however, these pillars no longer exist.

"Not content with a distant view, Denver people have always gone into the mountains for recreation." (Louisa Ward Arps, Denver In Slices, page 41)

And go into the mountains they did, especially with the establishment of the Denver Mountain Parks and the increasing availability of the automobile in the decade from 1910-1920. Denver had a chain of "picnic parks" extending all along Bear Creek Canyon from Morrison to Kittredge. Bear Creek virtually became Denver's own "municipal trout stream." When summer days in Denver became unbearably hot, visitors streamed up the road in Bear Creek Canyon (as they still do today) in search of cooler temperatures, clear cool water for wading and fishing, and grassy picnic spots under shady pine trees along the babbling brook.

Like the early visitors, we can reach the Bear Creek Parks today along now-paved Highway 74 west of Morrison. The highway winds up the canyon, passing park after park, including a Jefferson County Open

Space Park- Lair O' The Bear. The parks are generally small and confined to the banks of the creek. You can easily drive in and out of all the parks in a day. But why not take your time, pick out a park, and enjoy a leisurely picnic at one of these historic gems? It's just as fun to get cooled off in one of these parks today as it was back in 1914!

Perched along the banks of Bear Creek, Morrison Park's 20 acres were acquired in 1927. Its acreage today is included in the total acreage for Red Rocks Park since it is adjacent to it. Within Morrison Park's acreage is a Civilian Conservation Corps camp built in 1935. The still-preserved CCC camp in the western portion of Morrison Park serves today as the headquarters for the Denver Mountain Parks system, and is not open to the public. The CCC workers lived in the barracks-like buildings shown in the photo on the next page. Camp workers constructed the nearby Red Rocks Amphitheatre from 1936-1941. The Morrison CCC camp is one of the few remaining totally preserved CCC camps in the country, and it consists of several barracks, a dining hall, recreation hall, bathhouse, officer's quarters, infirmary, blacksmith shop, carpenter's shop, and machine shop.

Civilian Conservation Corps camp buildings in Morrison Park can be viewed just off the south side of Highway 74 across from Red Rocks Park gate 4.

Just a little farther west from Morrison Park on Highway 74 is Bear Creek Canyon Park. This is one of Denver's "conservation parks" where the land is protected from commercial development, and there are no developed park facilities. This park's 130 acres, acquired in 1928, stretches for four miles along Highway 74 from Morrison to Idledale and is only 400 feet wide. There are pullouts from the highway, which allow for picnics and fishing access.

While settlers found their way up the Bear Creek valley in the late 1860's, it would be a long time until they had a decent road up the canyon. The canyon was narrow and twisting, and subject to frequent floods. With the formation of the Denver Mountain Parks system in 1912, it soon became necessary to complete the loop road connecting the north parks (Lookout Mountain, Genesee, Fillius and Bergen) with all the south parks in Bear Creek Canyon. Thus, construction was begun on the Bear Creek Road in April of 1915 and was completed in December, 1915. Warwick Downing, writing in the Denver Municipal Facts March-April 1931 issue stated: "With the completion of such drive during the year, the success of the Mountain Parks became assured." However, local residents had to wait until 1940 for pavement to finally come along to settle the dust on the road.

BEAR CREEK CANON DRIVE.   DENVER MOUNTAIN PARKS.

What To Do In The Parks

Picnic
There are a number of picnic tables in Morrison Park. In Bear Creek Canyon, picnic areas are limited to the pullout areas on the highway. The descent to the creek from the highway is steep, so be sure to use caution to prevent slips and falls.

Fishing
Fishing is allowed in Bear Creek in both parks with a valid Colorado fishing license. The creek may be closed to fishing due to low water flow at times during the summer.

Tubing
Tubing is difficult because of large rocks and low stream flow in summer, but it is possible on stretches of Bear Creek.

Games
Morrison Park has a sand volleyball court and horseshoe pits.

Biking
Highway 74 provides a scenic route for cyclists, though traffic can be heavy at times.

Getaway 7- Starbuck Park

Getting There-

See the map on page 64. Heading west on Highway 74 through Bear Creek Canyon, you will round a curve and see a sign for the town of Idledale ahead. Turn immediately left before you reach the sign. Then take the right fork down to Bear Creek, and you will see the J.J.B. Benedict-designed well house (photo above) in Starbuck Park.

The Story Behind The Park

An early settlement grew up in 1866 just four miles west of Morrison in Bear Creek Canyon. It was variously called Joyland or Ida's Dale. John Starbuck acquired this site in 1906 and began selling lots in "Starbuck" for summer mountain cabins. In 1916 he donated 11 acres in Starbuck to Denver Mountain Parks. In 1938, residents changed the name of the town to Idledale. Early automobiles required frequent water refills in the radiator, so well houses such as the one in Starbuck Park were established along roads in Denver Mountain Parks.

What To Do In The Park
Picnic
Picnics are quite pleasant along the shaded creek in Starbuck Park.
Fishing
Fishing is allowed in the park with a Colorado fishing license.

Getaway 8- Little Park

Getting There-
See the map on page 64. Immediately west of Idledale on Highway 74 take the first left turn down the hill to Little Park. Like Starbuck Park, Little Park also has a stone well house designed by J.J.B. Benedict (background in photo above).

The Story Behind The Park
"Little" has nothing to do with the size of this park- with 400 acres it is one of the mid-sized Denver Mountain Parks. The land was donated by C.W. Little to Denver in 1917, but most of the park land is inaccessible on the steep hillside south across Bear Creek.

To get to Little Park today, travelers drive down a steep road to Bear Creek. The Civilian Conservation Corps relocated Highway 74 high above Bear Creek here in 1938 to help avoid flooding of the road. Also, the CCC built a stone and log footbridge over Bear Creek in

Little Park so that visitors could reach the steep slopes on the south side of the park where the CCC built two miles of trails up the mountain. Unfortunately, the bridge was destroyed by a flood soon after it was built, and the trail up the mountain could no longer be accessed. The area south of the creek remains inaccessible today, but master plans call for reconstruction of the trail up the mountain in the future. The octagonal-roofed well house, designed by J.J.B. Benedict and built in 1919, is the main feature in the park today.

What To Do In The Park

Picnic
You can have a picnic in the well house where it is dark and cool, or sit on the sunny banks of Bear Creek.

Hiking
There is a fairly large parking lot in Little Park which helps accommodate regional hikers. You can begin the Bear Creek Trail here, heading west to the Jefferson County Open Space Lair O' The Bear Park, about a mile to the west. The trail continues westward for several miles through Corwina Park and O'Fallon Park and ends at Pence Park (see map page 78).

Biking
The Bear Creek Trail is open to hiking and cycling, so this provides a nice alternative to biking on Highway 74.

Fishing
Fishing is allowed in the park with a Colorado fishing license.

Getaway 9- Corwina Park

Getting There-
See the map on page 64. Corwina Park is just west of Jefferson County's Lair O' The Bear Park on Highway 74. Heading west, Corwina Park is located in three sections: 1) there is a picnic area along Bear Creek on the right side of the road; 2) on the left side of the road there is a parking area for the stone shelter which is reached by a footbridge across Bear Creek; 3) a little further west, just beyond mile marker 11, turn left into a parking area for access to the Panorama Point Trail, a 1.5 mile hiking trail to the top of the mountain with great views of Mount Evans to the west.

The Story Behind The Park
The 298 acres for Corwina Park were acquired by Denver in 1916. The historic stone picnic shelter shown on the next page was built in 1918. The Panorama Point Trail (trailhead behind Corwina Park sign in photo above) in the westernmost section of the park was built by Volunteers for Outdoor Colorado. In 2000 they built the first segment joining Corwina Park with the Bear Creek Trail, and in 2001 they built the next segment to the top of the mountain.

The stone picnic shelter at Corwina Park was built in 1918.

What To Do In The Park

Picnic

Picnic tables are available in the three sections of the park, or just lay a blanket along Bear Creek. Restrooms are available in the eastern section.

Hiking

The Panorama Point Trail begins in the westernmost section of the park. This 1.5 mile trail is for hiking only, and leads to the top of the mountain where great views of Kittredge and Mount Evans are seen off to the west. You can join the Bear Creek Trail halfway up the Panorama Point Trail and hike it east or west to other Bear Creek Parks.

Biking

Cyclists are not allowed on the Panorama Point Trail. You will have to access the Bear Creek Trail from other parks to the east or west.

Fishing

Fishing is allowed in the park with a Colorado fishing license.

Getaway 10- O'Fallon Park

Getting There-

See the map on page 64. Just west of Corwina Park on Highway 74 you'll round a curve and see a tall stone chimney on the left. Take the next left turn into the park.

The Story Behind The Park

The stone chimney is a monument to Martin J. O'Fallon who donated 860 acres to Denver Mountain Parks in 1938. The chimney actually serves four different fireplaces separated by stone walls sloping down from the chimney. Each fireplace has stone benches next to it where picnickers could sit while cooking hot dogs in the fireplace or warming their hands on a cool day. The chimney originally had a roof extending over the fireplaces providing shelter for the picnickers. The fireplaces are no longer usable, but the tall structure is still a fine monument to one man's generous donation of park land.

Martin O'Fallon's gift allowed Denver to connect existing Pence Park and Corwina Park with O'Fallon Park in 1,487 contiguous acres, opening up the possibility of connecting trails between the three parks. In 2002, a multi-use trail (the Bear Creek Trail) was completed by Denver and Jefferson County linking the three parks as well as Lair O' The Bear Park and Little Park. Today, O'Fallon Park is Denver's most popular park on Bear Creek, and the throngs of visitors have created big problems for the park. Social trails and erosion of the stream bed by waders have seriously degraded the park. The sheer number of people in the park detracts from its quiet ambiance. If funding ever allows, Denver will have to take some serious steps to restore and preserve this special place.

Crowds flock to Bear Creek in O'Fallon Park on summer days.

What To Do In The Park

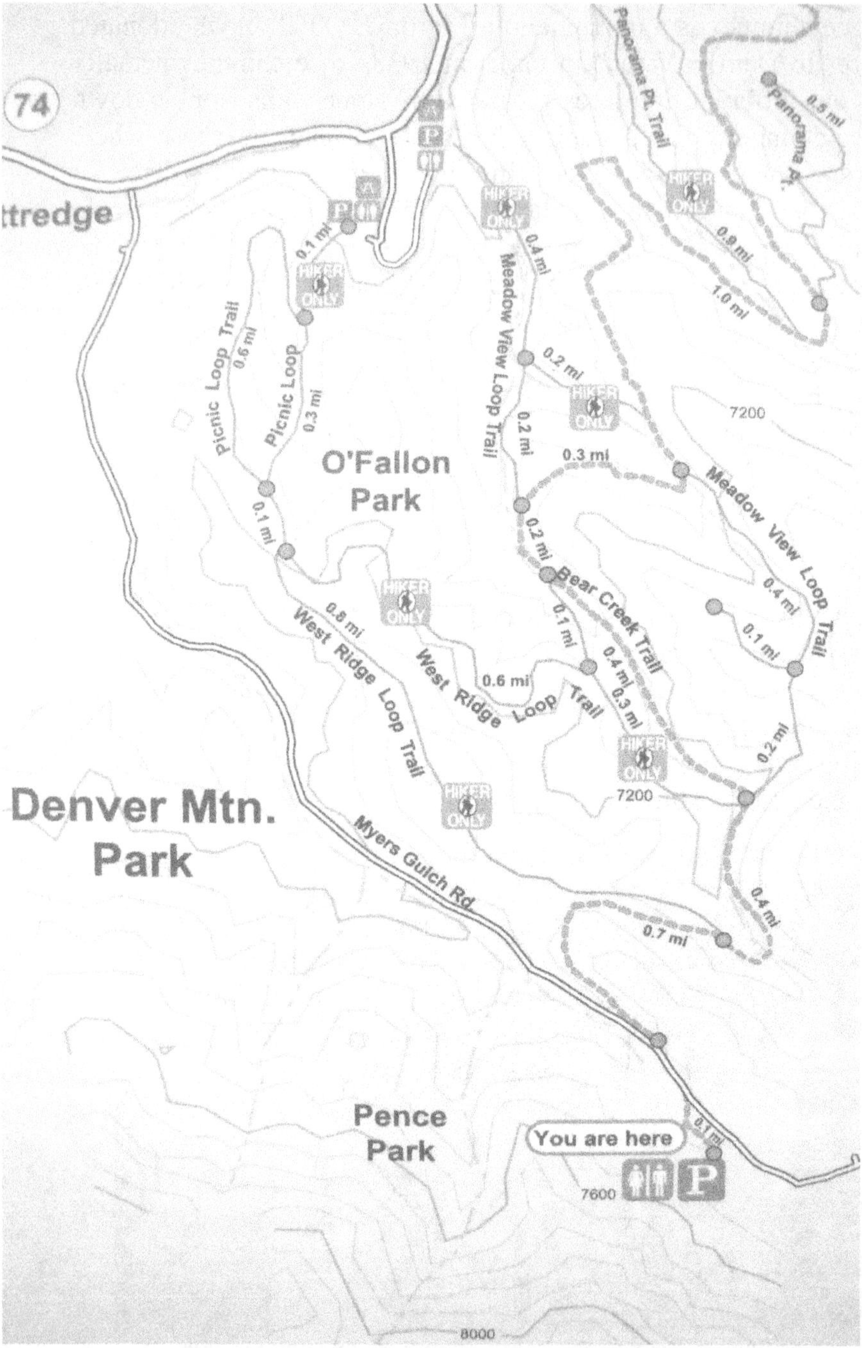

Hiking

Loop trails abound in O'Fallon Park, making great hikes for families with fairly short distances involved. The trails can be accessed from the picnic grounds on both the west and east sides (see map page 78). From the west picnic ground:
- Picnic Loop Trail- 1.1 miles
- West Ridge Loop Trail- 3.1 miles
From the east picnic ground:
- Meadow View Loop Trail- 2.4 miles

Hikers can connect from O'Fallon Park to Pence Park (2.1 miles) by hiking part of the Picnic Loop Trail to part of the West Ridge Loop Trail, and finishing up on the Bear Creek Trail and Myers Gulch Road. Hikers can connect from O'Fallon Park to Corwina Park (2.5 miles) by hiking part of the Meadow View Loop Trail to the connecting trail to the Bear Creek Trail, to the Panorama Point Trail down to Corwina Park.

Biking

Cyclists are allowed only on the Bear Creek Trail in O'Fallon Park. It is possible to ride the Bear Creek Trail all the way from Pence Park east to Little Park.

Picnic

There are picnic tables on both the east and west sides of O'Fallon Park, with restrooms on each side.

Games

O'Fallon Park has a softball field and a volleyball court.

Tubing and Wading

You'll see all kinds of floating devices on Bear Creek through O'Fallon Park including tubes, rafts, and kayaks, although limited stream flow in the summer limits coverage of much distance. Wading is a popular activity and the only way to keep people out of the water on hot summer days would be to fence off the entire creek.

Fishing

Fishing is possible, but not recommend in O'Fallon Park because of the large numbers of people wading in Bear Creek.

Getaway 11- Pence Park

Getting There-
See the map on page 64. Take Highway 74 west to the town of Kittredge and turn south on Myers Gulch Road. This will take you up the mountain to the Pence Park parking area.

The Story Behind The Park
John H. Myers farmed 160 acres of wheat and oats in this area of Bear Creek in the late 1860's. Eventually this land was purchased by Charles H. Kittredge in 1920, and the town was born. The 320 acres for Pence Park were acquired by Denver in 1914 and named after K.A. Pence, one of the original 1913 Denver Mountain Parks Commissioners. In 1937, a picnic site, hiking trail and sled run were built by CCC workers in the park. In 1939 they extended a trail to the top of Independence Mountain. Current master plans call for eventual reconstruction of that long since obliterated trail.

What To Do In The Park
A large parking lot serves hikers and bikers accessing the Bear Creek Trail (see map page 78). There is a picnic table and restroom.

Getaway 12- Deer Creek Canyon Park

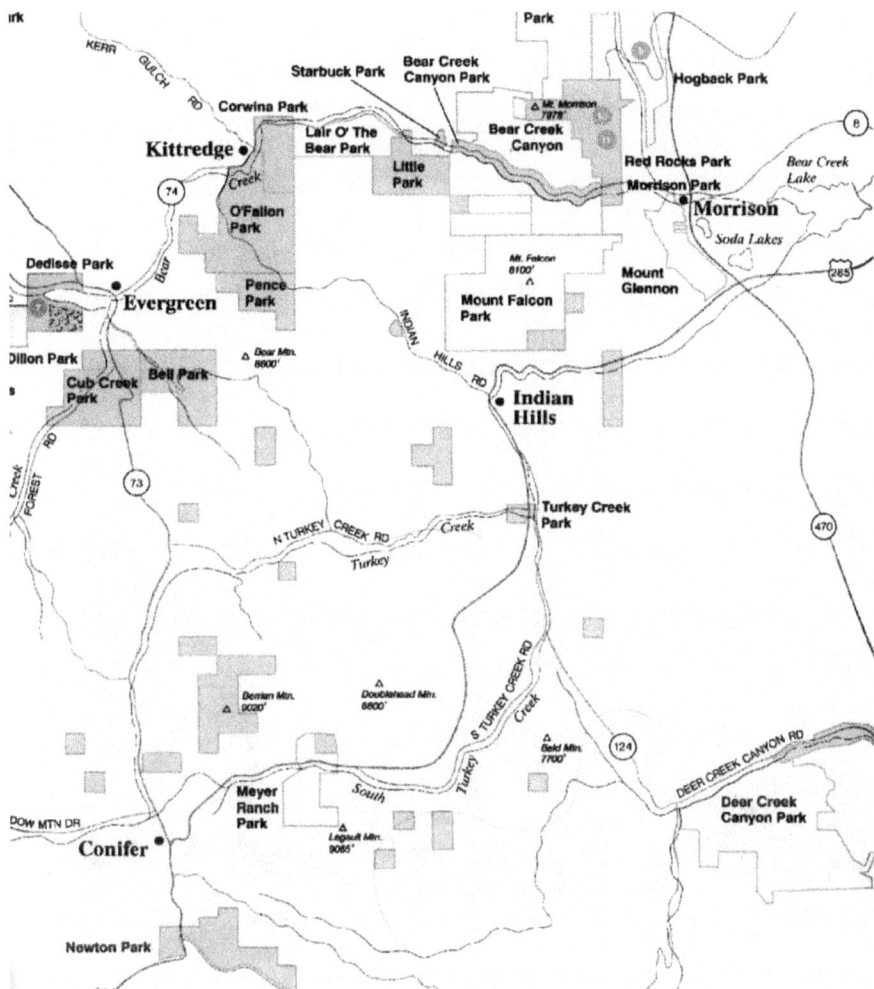

Getting There-

From Highway C-470, take the Wadsworth Exit south to Deer Creek Canyon Road (Road 124). Drive west and when the road forks, take the left turn. Drive west past the entrance to Lockheed Martin and you will be entering Denver Mountain Parks section of Deer Creek Canyon (shaded gray on the map above).

The Story Behind The Park

Deer Creek Canyon was settled in the 1880's when miners searched the upper canyon for gold and silver. When the mines played out, farms and ranches were developed at the mouth of Deer Creek Canyon. Denver acquired 90 acres in Deer Creek Canyon in 1918. The acreage is on both sides of Deer Creek Canyon Road. There are no facilities in the park, but there is a large parking pullout on the south side of the road. Essentially the preserved land serves as a buffer from encroaching subdivisions. This buffer provides shelter for birds and winter emergency range for elk. Jefferson County Open Space has a large park just west of Denver's land (map page 81).

Denver Mountain Parks preserves the land on both sides of the highway in Deer Creek Canyon.

What To Do In The Park

This is essentially a conservation area with no developed facilities. Just to the west, Jefferson County Open Space's Deer Creek Canyon Park has numerous hiking and mountain biking trails, along with picnic tables, shelters, and restrooms.

Getaway 13- Turkey Creek Park

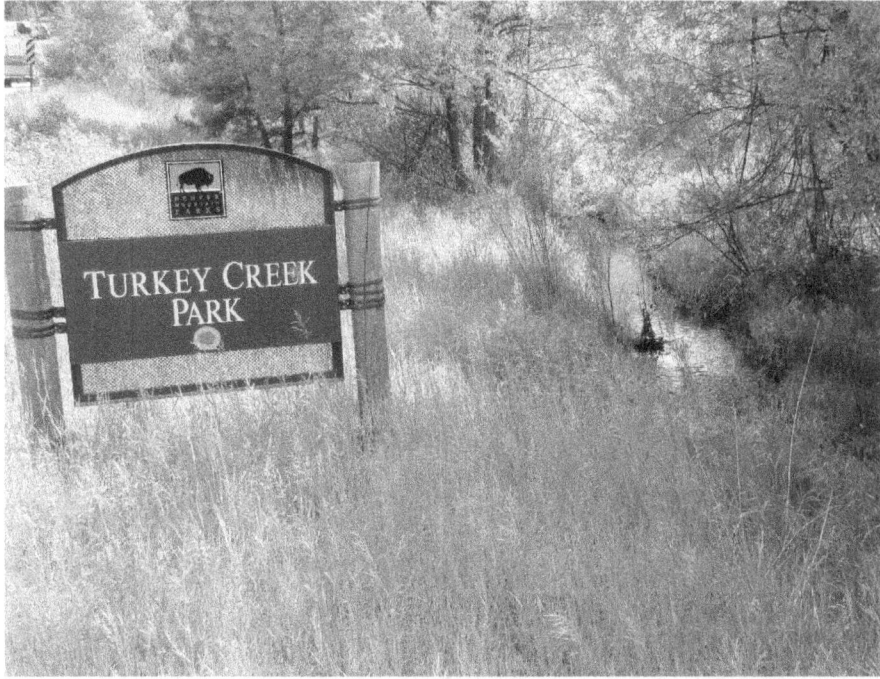

Getting There-
See the map on page 81. Continue west on Deer Creek Canyon Road to South Turkey Creek Road. Turn right on South Turkey Creek Road and proceed north to the park. Or take Highway 285 southwest out of Denver to the South Turkey Creek Road exit.

The Story Behind The Park
As four-lane U.S. Highway 285 blasts through the hogback just west of C-470 and climbs up Turkey Creek Canyon, it is hard to imagine the narrow, rocky wagon road that made its way up this canyon in the 1860's. While early explorers may have had dreams of finding gold and silver in the canyon, not much of the precious metals was found, so the early settlers survived on ranching, farming, and lumbering. John D. Parmalee arrived in Colorado in 1860, and operated a sawmill at the junction of Parmalee Gulch and Turkey Creek. The map on page 81 shows the intersection of Parmalee Gulch Road (now also called Indian Hills Road) with Highway 285. Parmalee was granted a

wagon road charter along Turkey Creek from 1866-1886. He charged the going rate for tolls on his road- $1.00 per wagon, with 25 cents additional for other animal-drawn carts, and 5 cents additional for each mule, horse, cattle or human, with the exception that people gained free passage to attend a place of worship or a funeral.

Denver acquired Turkey Creek's 61 acres in 1914, but the park was not constructed until 1927 to serve as the gateway to the southern loop of the Denver Mountain Parks. The park is bisected by Highway 285- the picnic area is on the east side of the highway, and the west side is undeveloped wild land consisting of high rocky ridges with large ponderosa pines.

349 TINYTOWN—THE TOY VILLAGE IN TURKEY CREEK CAÑON

DENVER MOUNTAIN PARKS, COLORADO   5655-29

Just to the north of Turkey Creek Park on South Turkey Creek Road is Tiny Town. George Turner developed his miniature village here on the banks of South Turkey Creek in 1915 to amuse his young daughter. By 1920, the town had grown so large that Turner opened it up to the public. The WPA Guide to 1930's Colorado stated: "Here, built to scale, one inch to a foot, are stores, dwellings, a filling station, a church facing a park, a broadcasting station with aerial towers, a large terracotta office building, a railroad station, and an old-fashioned river steamboat on a diminutive pond" (page 391). By

84

1924, as many as 20,000 people per year drove up from Denver to see the sights of Tiny Town.

Tiny Town has been damaged by many floods and fires over the years. In 1969 a flood on South Turkey Creek completely destroyed the town. In 1972, Lyle Fulkerson, a model train buff, began to rebuild Tiny Town. Fulkerson, however, died in 1977, and Tiny Town fell into disrepair and closed again. Finally in 1989 the non-profit Tiny Town Foundation was formed to preserve the town for the future. Today, Tiny Town has nearly 100 buildings, and an operating 15" wide steam engine pulling visitors 5/8 mile around the town and over trestles. There is also a railroad roundhouse and depot. The maximum grade of the rail line is 3%, and one steam engine can consume 140 pounds of coal and 100 - 150 gallons of water on a busy day. Tiny Town is open for the summer season, and often counts over 100,000 visitors per year. Despite the postcard caption on page 84, Tiny Town has never been a Denver Mountain Park, but it is near Turkey Creek Park.

What To Do In The Park

Picnic
South Turkey Creek Park offers picnic tables and a restroom.

Scenic Drive
The drive from Deer Creek Canyon Road up and over the mountains to South Turkey Creek Road is steep and winding. Combine the drive with a picnic at Turkey Creek Park for a nice 1/2 day outing.

Biking
Cyclists can leave their cars on Deer Creek Canyon Road at the parking areas just west of Wadsworth Blvd., and then begin the long ascent up the canyon to Turkey Creek. Automobile and bicycle traffic can both be heavy at times.

Tiny Town
A visit to Tiny Town is a delight for both children and adults. Call 303-697-6829 for information or go to www.tinytownrailroad.com.

Getaway 14- Newton Park

Getting There-

See the map on page 81. To reach Newton Park, head south on Highway 285 from Turkey Creek Park to Conifer. South of Conifer turn left (east) on Foxton Road to the three entrances for Newton Park.

The Story Behind The Park

Heading southwest on Highway 285 on your trip to Newton Park, you will first come to Meyer Ranch Open Space Park (Jefferson County Open Space) and a large meadow with a lovely Victorian house and barn. This meadow was first occupied by Duncan McIntyre and his family, immigrants from Canada, in the 1860's. They filed for a homestead here, and built a log cabin and barn (still standing to the right of the house in the photo on page 87) to serve their hay ranch. In 1883 Louis Ramboz bought 480 acres from McIntyre and ran a timber, hay and cattle business. In 1889 Ramboz built "Midway

House" (the current home) to serve as a hotel on the stage coach line between Denver and Leadville. Norman and Ethel Meyer bought the home and the ranch in 1950. In 1986 they sold the ranch (524 acres) to Jefferson County Open Space, but kept the home for their residence, where the family still resides. Mary Helen Crain, in her book A Circle of Pioneers (page 34), interviewed Mrs. Meyer about the history of the home. Mrs. Meyer stated that when new plumbing was put in the house, the plumber found a board marked in pencil: "This house is been built by Joseph Grauffel of the city of Denver for Mr. Louis Ramboz. Is been commenced in March, 1889 and finished in October of the same year."

Myer house (left) and barn(to the right of the house).

When you turn on Foxton Road to Newton Park, you will find that there are three separate entrances to the park, leading to three separate picnic sites. The 431 acres for the park were donated to Denver in two portions, one in 1939, and one in 1962. The land was donated from the family ranch of James Q. Newton (father of Quigg Newton, mayor of Denver from 1945-1951). The picnic shelters are obviously

1960's - 1970's designs, which pay no attention whatsoever (see photo below) to the historic designs of other buildings in Denver Mountain Parks.

Shelter at the Commissioners picnic site in Newton Park. Compare to the historic shelters at Genesee Park (page 61) and Corwina Park (page 75).

From west to east the three picnic sites are designated the Juvenile Site, Commissioners Site, and Stromberg site. Each site has a picnic shelter with potable water, electricity, restrooms and large recreation areas including softball fields, volleyball courts and horseshoe pits. There are also large grills and fire pits. All three sites are available by reservation for large groups only. Unfortunately, the park is not otherwise open for individual use. Newton Park has great possibilities for the future if funding can be obtained. The three sites can easily be linked by trails. Ropes challenge courses could be added, as well as overnight tent camping for groups of students from the inner city. The sites could be opened to the public on weekdays, when they are seldom used by groups.

What To Do In The Park

Softball field behind the picnic shelter at Commissioners site.

Picnic
Large groups may reserve one of the picnic shelters at Newton Park by calling 720-913-0700.

Games
Games for large groups are encouraged with softball fields and volleyball courts.

Hiking
Hiking is limited to short social trails around each picnic site. There are no connecting trails between the sites.

Group campfire circle at Commissioners Site.

Getaway 15- Cub Creek/Dillon Park

Getting There-
See the map on page 81. From Newton Park return to Conifer on Highway 285, and then take Highway 73 north to Cub Creek Park. From Morrison, take Highway 74 west to Evergreen, and then take Highway 73 south to Cub Creek. The picnic tables in Cub Creek Park can be reached by turning from Highway 73 on to Brook Forest Road.

The Story Behind The Park
Cub Creek's 549 acres were acquired by Denver in 1922. In 1960, 160 acres within Cub Creek Park were dedicated to honor Frank C. Dillon, and that portion of the park is marked with a sign (below).

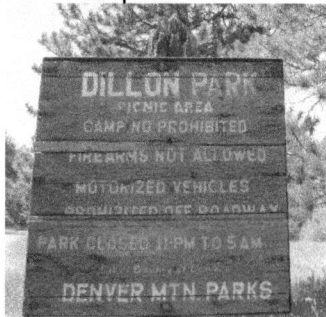

From Conifer To Cub Creek Park

Highway 73 north from Conifer passes through a very historic area. Look for a striking yellow barn on the right side of the highway at the intersection of Barkley Road. John and Jeannette Mullen ordered this entire barn from the Sears Catalog in 1918. It was a Dutch-style barn made of cypress siding. Sears shipped the barn pieces by rail to Pine, Colorado, where it was then loaded on wagons and hauled north to Conifer. Neighbors helped the Mullens piece together this huge barn, which is 34 feet x 44 feet, comprising about 5,000 square feet. The barn has three levels, with carriages and wagons stored in the basement level, horses kept on the main level, and hay kept in the upper level. The hay loft had a hardwood floor, and the upper levels of the barn were often used for social purposes in Conifer, including square dances in the loft.

The yellow barn just north of Conifer on Highway 73.

The well house (above) in front of the barn dates from the 1860's. It was at the intersection of the Bergen Park road and the South Turkey Creek Road. This junction was called Bradford Junction, named after Robert Bradford who built the road from here north to connect to Bergen Park. The well was necessary to water the animals (horses, mules, and oxen) which pulled wagons over the roads. At the junction, Bradford built a hotel, saloon, grocery and restaurant. This was the precursor to Conifer. Mary Helen Crain in her book (page 21) states: "Douglas Hamer came to live at the Junction around 1900, and was impressed by the pines heavily laden with cones, and changed the name to Conifer."

What To Do In Cub Creek/Dillon Park

Picnic
The picnic area along Brook Forest Road is shaded and very peaceful.

Scenic Drive
One of Denver Mountain Parks famous circle routes can be taken to Cub Creek Park by driving west from Morrison on Highway 74, south from Evergreen to Cub Creek on Highway 73, further south to Conifer, and returning to Denver on Highway 285.

Getaway 16- Bell Park

Mt. Evans towers on the horizon west of Bell Park.

Getting There-
See the map on page 81. From Conifer take Highway 73 north past Cub Creek Park and then turn right (east) on South Little Cub Creek Road. Then turn left on Stanley Park Road. When there are no more houses, you are in Bell Park. There are no signs marking the park. From Evergreen drive south on Highway 73 to South Little Cub Creek Road and turn left. Then turn left again on Stanley Park Road.

The Story Behind The Park
Denver acquired Bell Park's 480 acres in 1915. It is essentially a conservation park and there have never been any facilities developed in the park.

What To Do In The Park
Drive to Bell Park to admire the magnificent views of Mount Evans. Pick out a spot for a picnic with a view!

Getaway 17- Fillius Park

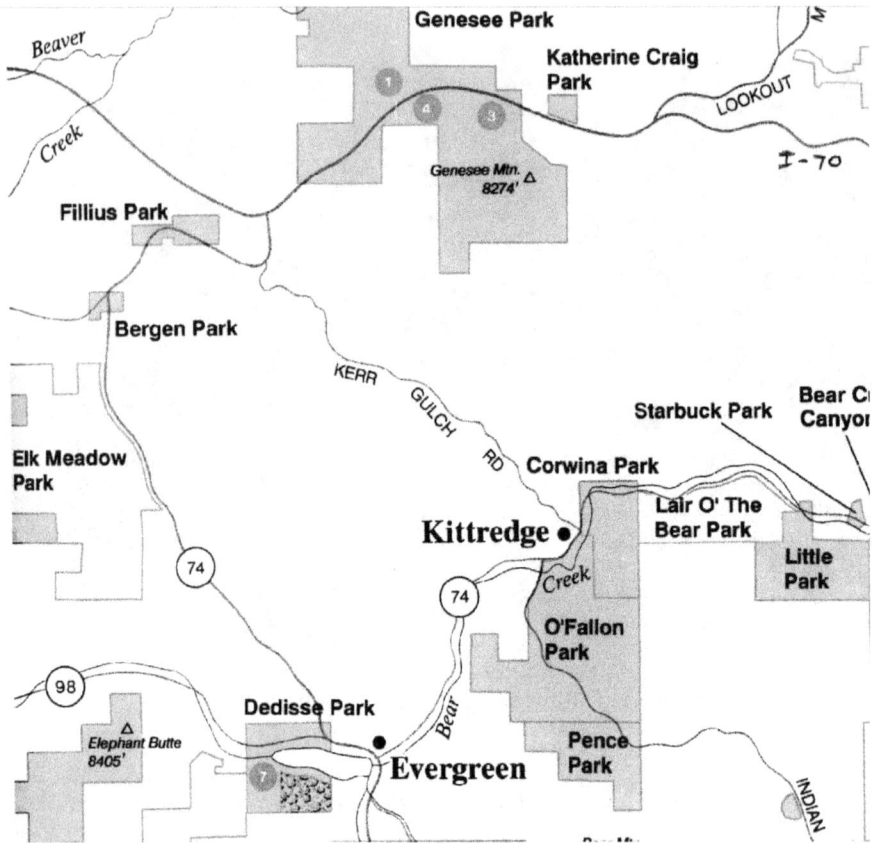

Getting There-
Take I-70 west to the Evergreen Parkway exit (Highway 74) and head south beyond the first stoplight. At the second stoplight, turn right on Bergen Parkway and immediately into Fillius Park.

The Story Behind The Park
The 107 acres for Fillius Park were acquired by Denver in 1914. The park was named after Jacob Fillius, a member of the Denver Parks Board. Besides its natural beauty of rolling hills, meadows and pines, the most striking feature of Fillius Park is the picnic shelter designed by Denver architect J.J.B. Benedict. This is perhaps Benedict's most unique shelter, with its patterns of different colored stones, stone buttresses, round windows, and timber arches. It was built in 1918,

Fillius Park picnic shelter designed by J.J.B. Benedict

and the north side has an open arch with views facing toward the Continental Divide. Today, Soda Creek Road bisects the park, with this shelter and picnic tables on the southeast side, and an open meadow and more picnic tables in the western section.

The Soda Creek Road was constructed in 1873 to connect Bergen Park with the Colorado Central Railroad station at Beaver Brook (where Beaver Brook joins Clear Creek- illustration page 96). With mining booming in the Central City area, it was important that the farmers and ranchers of the Bergen Park area have access for shipping their products to Central City by rail. The Soda Creek Road was their link to this vital market. One of the early settlers along Soda Creek Road was J.J. Clarke who obtained 350 acres there in 1878. He homesteaded land which is included in the present Fillius Park. About a mile north he built a log cabin on his land. Clarke owned a butcher shop and grocery in Central City, so he used his ranch to fatten cattle for his butcher shop.

BEAVER BROOK, C. C. R. R.

In 1920 Clarke sold his ranch to Lucius Humphrey, a Denver newspaperman. Humphrey lived in the home with his wife Hazel and daughter Hazel Lou.   During the 1920's Hazel Lou and her mother operated a trading post adjacent to Fillius Park which sold groceries, drinks, and souvenirs to the numerous campers arriving in the park.

Hazel Humphrey and her daughter Hazel Lou sold concessions to Fillius Park visitors from this cabin in the 1920's.

What To Do In The Park

Picnic

Have a picnic in the historic 1918 Benedict shelter. Picnic tables are also available in the section of the park west of Soda Creek Road.

Scenic Drive

Fillius Park was established as a gateway park on the drive west to Squaw Pass and Echo Lake, and as a picnic stop on the circle route (see map page 13) of Mountain Parks. This scenic drive can be driven today by taking I-70 west through Genesee Park, and then south on Highway 74 to Fillius, Bergen, and Dedisse Parks, and then east from Evergreen on Highway 74 through the Bear Creek Canyon Parks to Morrison.

Humphrey Memorial Park and Museum

The Humphrey home, located at 620 Soda Creek Road, about a mile north of Fillius Park, is preserved as a museum and it's well worth a visit to this historic home. The Humphrey family continued to occupy the home until the last living family member, Hazel Lou, died in 1995. Hazel Lou envisioned that her ranch and home would someday be a museum. She left a trust fund and a will that created what is now the Humphrey Memorial Park and Museum. Tours of the museum are conducted, and there is a tea room which hosts special events. Go to www.hmpm.org for more information.

The historic Humphrey home contains an incredible collection of memorabilia gathered by the family during their worldwide travels.

Getaway 18- Bergen Park

Getting There-
See the map on page 94. Take I-70 west to the Evergreen Parkway exit (Highway 74). Go south on Highway 74 to Bergen Park. Turn left at the RTD Park-n-Ride and then turn right into the park.

The Story Behind The Park
Bergen Park is deceptive. It's only 25 acres and, driving by, it looks like a congested little spot surrounded by highways and an RTD Park-n-Ride lot. Don't be fooled. Take a few minutes to go into the park. You may see elk grazing near the J.J.B. Benedict stone shelter. You'll definitely feel the coolness of the shade under the ponderosa pines. It's a great place to go for a picnic on the way west to Mount Evans just as it was in 1915 when the park was acquired from a donation by Oscar N. Johnson. The park is named for Thomas Bergen, an Illinois farmer, who was the first settler in the Bergen Park area in 1859.

Bypassing the Cherry Creek gold rush in Denver, Bergen headed west with his wife Judith and three children to establish a cattle ranch. He built a home which he also used as a hotel for passing travelers. The WPA Guide to 1930's Colorado observed that Bergen served "50 Cent meals ('never higher and never lower, whatever the times,') noted throughout the territory." Bergen made a good living serving guests and exchanging fresh ox teams for miners' worn out oxen as they were going back and forth from the Clear Creek mining region. By the mid 1870's, the arrival of the railroad in Clear Creek and Morrison threatened to put Bergen out of business. So he sold out and moved to Morrison, where he established a successful trout hatchery.

The beautiful picnic shelter in Bergen Park (above) was designed by J.J.B. Benedict and built in 1917. It was constructed from white quartz stone and timber. He also designed the well house in the park which was built of the same material.

Elk graze near the well house in Bergen Park.

What To Do In The Park

Picnic
Bergen is a delightful picnic park. Plan a stop here on the way to or from a drive to Mount Evans.

Wildlife Viewing
Bergen Park provides elk and mule deer habitat, and serves as a refuge for elk herds crossing under the Highway 74 bridge just to the south of the park. You may see elk grazing in the park in the summer.

Hiking
A regional multi-use trail, the Pioneer Trail, runs along the western edge of Bergen Park and goes 5.5 miles south to Dedisse Park, Evergreen Lake, and downtown Evergreen.

Biking
The Pioneer Trail is great for biking also.

Getaway 19- Dedisse Park

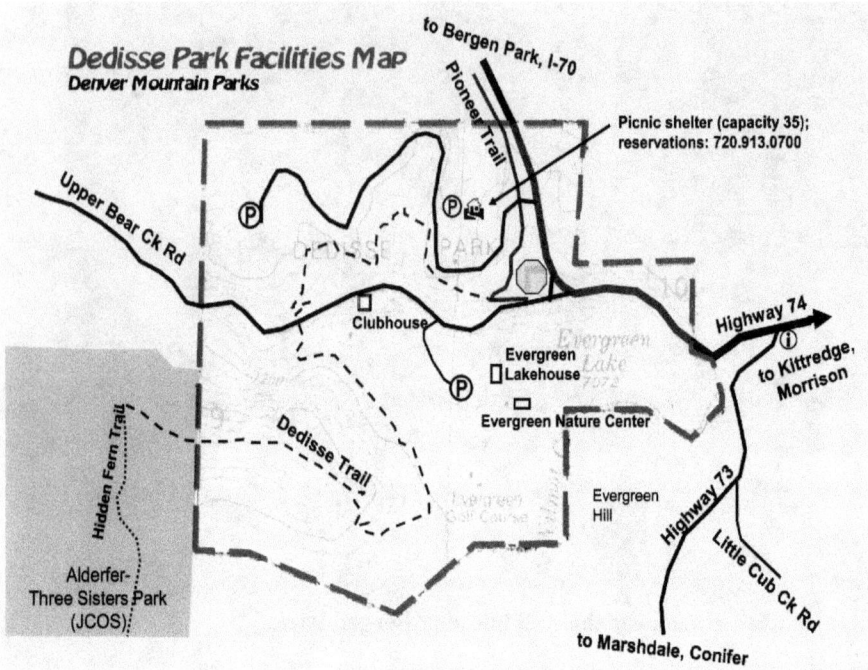

Dedisse Park Facilities Map
Denver Mountain Parks

to Bergen Park, I-70

Pioneer Trail

Picnic shelter (capacity 35);
reservations: 720.913.0700

Upper Bear Ck Rd

Clubhouse

Highway 74

to Kittredge, Morrison

Evergreen Lakehouse

Evergreen Nature Center

Hidden Fern Trail

Dedisse Trail

Evergreen Hill

Highway 73

Little Cub Ck Rd

Alderfer-
Three Sisters Park
(JCOS)

to Marshdale, Conifer

Getting There-
Take I-70 west to the Evergreen Parkway exit (Highway 74). Go
south on Highway 74 past Bergen Park to Dedisse Park

The Story Behind The Park
This large 420 acre park was acquired by Denver from the pioneering
Dedisse family in 1919. French immigrant Julian Dedisse and his
wife Mary Ann, homesteaded this area in 1869, establishing a hay
ranch in the broad meadow which is now filled by Evergreen Lake.
Today, Dedisse Park is bisected by Upper Bear Creek Road, with the
hilly northern section of the park containing a picnic shelter and
tables, and the broad valley to the south containing Evergreen Lake
and Evergreen Golf Course (map above). Denver wanted to control
flooding on Bear Creek which frequently wreaked havoc on its Bear
Creek Parks, as well as the small towns in the valley. Obtaining the
Dedisse ranch allowed Denver to build a dam on Bear Creek to
control the flooding. Also, as stated in the issue of Denver Municipal

Facts for April-May, 1920: "A sixty-five acre lake would be created where Denver's residents and visitors may enjoy trout fishing, boating, and camping." The creation of the dam and lake in 1927, certainly achieved this goal, and while no camping is allowed here today, Dedisse Park is always crammed with fishermen, picnickers, boaters, hikers, and golfers on any summer day. Winter days see ice fishing and ice skating on the lake. The popularity of the lake and the park is almost too great, as overcrowding and lack of parking spaces are nearly always a problem.

15721. Dam and Lake at Evergreen in Bear Creek Canon, Denver Mountain Parks

Denver built the first mountain golf course in Colorado in 1921, with the construction of nine holes at the west end of the Dedisse valley, beyond where waters of the future Evergreen Lake would extend. In 1927, Troutdale-In-The Pines hotel/resort owner Henry Sidles donated land to Denver for an additional nine holes for the Evergreen Golf Course, on the condition that the complete 18-hole course be built and maintained by Denver as a course open to the public forever. Today, the golf course and clubhouse, whiled owned by Denver, are managed by a concessionaire. The octagonal clubhouse (photo next page) was constructed in 1925. It was designed by Denver architect J.J.B. Benedict, and was constructed of logs for the sum of $9,000.

Evergreen Golf Course Clubhouse and Keys On The Green Restaurant which serves golfers and the general public.

In the late 1930's, the Civilian Conservation Corps constructed several facilities in Dedisse Park. In the northern section of the park they built roads up the hill, three separate picnic sites, and the stone shelter pictured below.

Warming hut/boathouse built by the CCC on the south shore of Evergreen Lake.

The warming hut on the south shore of Evergreen Lake served ice skaters in the winter, and offered boat rentals in the summer. In 1993, it was replaced by the 5,000 square foot Lake House (photo below), built for $1.1 million by the Evergreen Park and Recreation District on land leased from the City and County of Denver.

What To Do In The Park

Picnic

Enjoy a picnic in the historic stone shelter in the northern section of the park (call 720-913-0700 for reservations) or along the shore of Evergreen Lake in the southern section of the park.

Hiking

The Pioneer Trail from Bergen Park enters the northern section of Dedisse Park, and from that point hikers can join the Dedisse Trail (see map page 102) to the southern section of the park past Evergreen Golf Course, and on to Alderfer/Three Sisters Park (Jefferson County Open Space). There is also a 1.3 mile loop trail around Evergreen Lake.

Golf

Call 303-674-6351 for tee time reservations at Evergreen Golf Course.

Boating
Small boats can be rented at the old boathouse on the south shore of Evergreen Lake. Since 2008, the Evergreen Nature Center, operated by the Evergreen Audubon Society, has also been housed in this building.

Fishing
With a Colorado fishing license, you may fish in Evergreen Lake year-round. Ice fishing is popular in the winter.

325--Evergreen Hill Reflected in the Lake at Evergreen Bear Creek Cañon

Denver Mountain Parks, Colorado

Ice Skating
Ice skating is also very popular at Evergreen Lake in the winter. Skates can be rented at the Lake House, and there is a small fee collected for skating on the lake.

Elk Viewing
There is a resident herd of elk in the valley which can often be seen grazing on the grass of Evergreen Golf Course.

Getaway 20- Echo Lake Park

Denver Mountain Parks

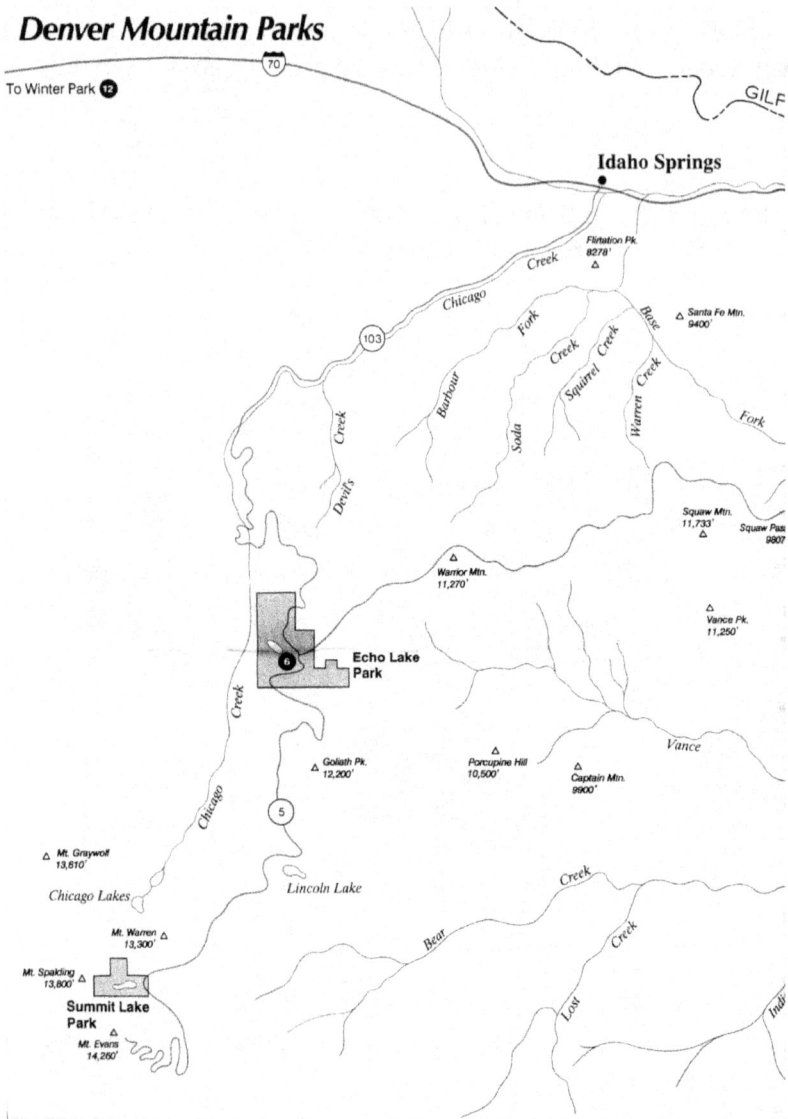

70

To Winter Park 12

GILF

Idaho Springs
●

Flirtation Pk.
8278'
△

Chicago   Creek

103

△ Santa Fe Mtn.
9400'

Fork

Barbour   Squirrel Creek

Creek

Warren Creek

Blue

Creek

Soda

Fork

Devils

Squaw Mtn.
11,733'
△   Squaw Pass
9807

△
Warrior Mtn.
11,270'

△
Vance Pk.
11,250'

**Echo Lake
Park**
6

Creek   Vance

△
Porcupine Hill
10,500'

△ Goliath Pk.
12,200'

△
Captain Mtn.
9900'

Chicago

5

△ Mt. Graywolf
13,610'

Chicago Lakes   Lincoln Lake   Creek

Creek

Bear

Mt. Warren △
13,300'

Lost

Indi

Mt. Spalding △
13,800'

**Summit Lake
Park**
△
Mt. Evans
14,260'

Getting There-

Take I-70 west to Idaho Springs, and then take Highway 103 south to
Echo Lake. Or take I-70 west to the Evergreen Parkway exit and go
south on Highway 74 to Bergen Park, and then west on Highway 103
to Echo Lake. Whichever way you go, take the other way back to
complete a beautiful scenic loop drive.

15650. Echo Lake, Colorado, Denver Mountain Parks

The Story Behind The Park

With its picturesque lodge, towering peaks, and shimmering lake, Echo Lake has the feel of a national park. In fact, Denver wanted Echo Lake and Mount Evans to be a national park, but settled for a Mountain Park in Arapaho National Forest when the Forest Service agreed to build the road from Bergen Park to Squaw Pass (completed in 1919), to Echo Lake (completed in 1920), and on to the top of Mount Evans (completed in 1931). Denver acquired 616 acres at Echo Lake in 1920 for its mountain park.

SCENE AT ECHO LAKE ON MT. EVANS ROAD, COLORADO

The J.J.B. Benedict designed Echo Lake Lodge (above) was built from 1926 -1927. It originally served as a hotel for guests, with rooms on the second level. There was a large lounge on the first floor surrounding a huge fireplace (below). Today, the second floor rooms are reserved for staff lodging, and the lounge area has been turned into a gift shop. Unfortunately, the fireplace is completely surrounded by trinkets and is very difficult to see. On the other hand, the beautiful dining room still exists, and serves wonderful meals for hikers, bikers, and Mount Evans travelers. The Lodge underwent extensive renovation in 2011, with rotted logs on the exterior replaced, and cracks filled with epoxy. Denver Mountain Parks master plan envisions the lodge being open in the future for winter recreational activities.

The picnic shelter (above) at Echo Lake was built in 1924. It was constructed of local stone and features four handsome arches. Just north of the shelter is the old Concession Stand which was also built in 1924. It rented ice skates and sold food back in the early days.

The dining room at Echo Lake Lodge still serves meals daily during summer.

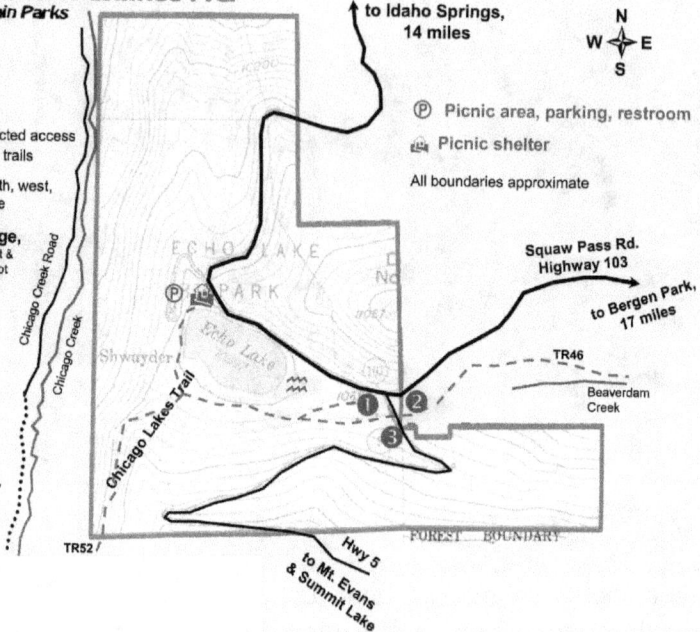

Echo Lake Park Facilities Map
Denver Mountain Parks

to Idaho Springs,
14 miles

N
W ✦ E
S

Ⓟ Picnic area, parking, restroom

🏠 Picnic shelter

All boundaries approximate

〰〰 Wetland, restricted access
TR46 Forest Service trails

Fishing access on north, west,
and south sides of lake

❶ **Echo Lake Lodge,**
historic bldg; restaurant &
gift shop open May-Sept
303.567.2138

❷ **Forest Service**
campground

❸ **Mt. Evans**
fee station
Fees charged to
access facilities on
Mt. Evans Road
Information: Clear
Creek Ranger District,
303.567.2901

Chicago Creek Road

Chicago Creek

ECHO LAKE
PARK

Shwayder

Echo Lake

Ohicago Lakes Trail

Squaw Pass Rd.
Highway 103

to Bergen Park,
17 miles

TR46

Beaverdam
Creek

FOREST BOUNDARY

TR52

Hwy 5
to Mt. Evans
& Summit Lake

What To Do In The Park

Picnic
Choose either the large picnic shelter (call 720-913-0700 for reservations) or a site along the lakeshore for a relaxing time.

Hiking
The popular Chicago Lakes Trail can be accessed from either Echo Lake Lodge or the picnic shelter on the lake. This is a fairly strenuous day hike as it is five miles down to the lakes, and then you'll be faced with the rugged hike back up the mountain at the end of the day. Another popular hike, the Captain Mountain trail, starts at the Forest Service campground and heads east to Captain Mountain and the Mount Evans State Wildlife Area (see map on page 116).

Fishing
Fishing is a year-round activity at Echo Lake, with a Colorado fishing license required.

Winter Sports
Cross country skiing and snowshoeing are popular along the Mount Evans road which is closed in the winter.

112

Getaway 21- Summit Lake Park and Mount Evans

Getting There-
See the map on page 108. From Echo Lake Park, drive south on the Mount Evans Highway (Highway 5) to Summit Lake Park, and then on to the summit of Mount Evans.

The Story Behind The Park
Construction of the road up Mount Evans proceeded from Echo Lake to Summit Lake in 1923, and Denver acquired Summit Lake Park's 162 acres in 1924. The stone shelter (below) in the park was designed by J.J.B. Benedict, and completed in 1926.

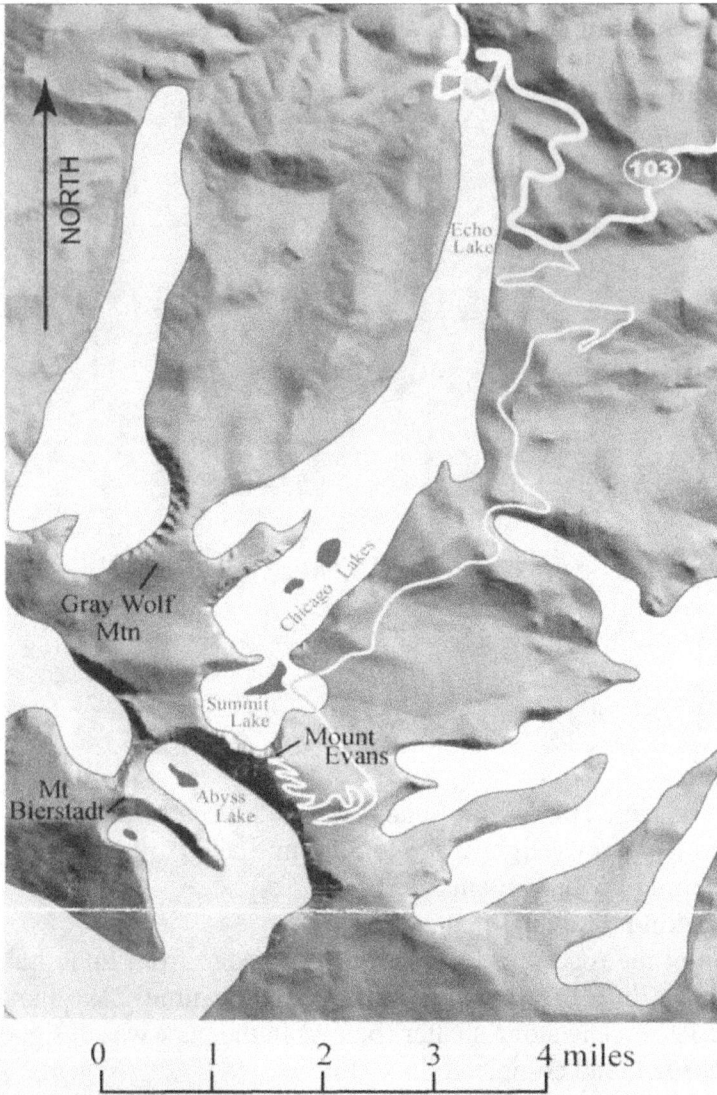

U.S. Forest Service map of glaciation at Mount Evans.

The story of Summit Lake and the Chicago Lakes Basin is one of glaciation. There were two glacial eras on Mount Evans, the first from 120,000 to 170,000 years ago, and the second from 12,000 to 30,000 years ago. These periods of glaciation filled the area around Mount Evans with ice that was 800 to 1,000 feet thick (seen as the white areas on the map above). The weight of the ice gouged out deep U-shape valleys where lakes (black on map) formed after the

Chicago Lakes as seen from the overlook trail from the Summit Lake parking lot.

glaciers melted. The Chicago Lakes (above) are in a U-shape valley just below Summit Lake, and Summit Lake is in a cirque- a bowl-shaped depression made by the ice.

Highway 5, the Mount Evans Road (see the map on page 116), was completed in 1931. The road connected Denver's Echo Lake Park and Summit Lake Park with the top of Mount Evans. The parking lot on the peak is at 14,130 feet, while the peak summit is a few feet higher at 14,264 feet. The road is generally open to the top from Memorial Day to Labor Day. The road is usually open as far as Summit Lake until mid-September, when snows and high winds close the road until next May. Driving up the road is an experience not to be missed. The small fee charged at the entrance station is well worth it, as it helps fund upkeep of the road, restrooms, and parking areas. A portion of the fees also goes to Denver for upkeep and improvements at Summit Lake Park.

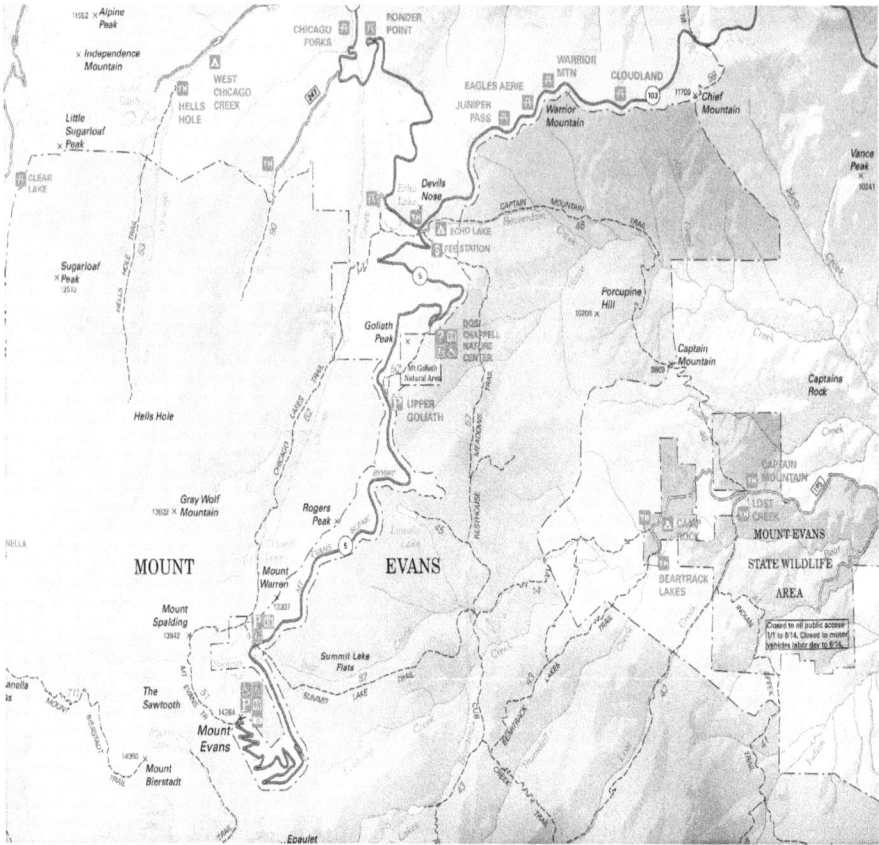

U.S. Forest Service map of Mount Evans Highway (Highway 5).

At the summit of Mount Evans the Crest House was built from 1940-1941. It was two stories tall with slanting walls of glass and stone. It consisted of a coffee shop, gift shop, restrooms, and sleeping rooms for employees. It was nearly destroyed in the winter of 1943, when vicious winds blew in the windows and filled the building with snow drifts up to five feet deep. After World War II, Crest House served happy customers on the top of Mount Evans until the dreadful day of September 1, 1979, when it was destroyed by a propane explosion. It has never reopened, but thanks to proceeds from entry fees on the Mount Evans Road, the Forest Service has stabilized and restored the remains, so that visitors today can go into the structure, walk through it, and even have a picnic on the picnic tables inside. Crest House was designed by architect Edwin Francis.

Crest House on Mount Evans in the 1940's.

Leslie Wildeson of the State Historic Preservation Office wrote about the Crest House: "The design is unique for its interesting combination of organic, futuristic, and art modern elements that reflect not only its time period but illustrate an adaptation to its western mountain-top setting." (from a sign at Crest House)

The remains of Crest House today. Compare the three windows in the middle with those in the photograph above.

Just beyond the remains of Crest House to the east is the S.F. Meyer-Womble Observatory of the University of Denver. The modern telescope in the observatory was installed in 1996, but a cosmic ray laboratory was constructed there in 1935. It was housed in an A-frame building designed by Burnham Hoyt, who also designed Red Rocks Amphitheatre and Denver Public Library. Hiking the trail from the parking lot to the summit of Mount Evans allows a good view of the observatory (above), and Summit Lake (below).

Summit Lake from the top of Mount Evans.

What To Do In The Park

Scenic Drive

A drive along North America's highest paved roadway to the summit of Mount Evans is an exhilarating experience not to be missed. The road to the summit is only open from Memorial Day to Labor Day, so plan accordingly. Starting at Echo Lake at 10,600 feet elevation in the ecological Subalpine Zone, the road climbs to the Alpine Zone (the treeless zone) at Summit Lake with its altitude of 12,830 feet. The change is quite noticeable as you drive from the heavily forested Echo Lake area up to the Mount Goliath area (at 11,540 feet) with its stunted and bent bristlecone pine trees, to Summit Lake which has no trees at all. Driving the Mount Evans Road seems very much like driving through a National Park with its spectacular mountain views and abundant wildlife. In addition to elk and mountain goats, you are likely to see bighorn sheep, marmots, pikas and birds including hawks and eagles. Allow at least an hour for a leisurely drive to the top, with stops along the way.

Mt. Goliath Natural Area preserves 160 acres of bristlecone pine trees for observation. The Dos Chappell Nature Center has interpretive displays.

Mountain Goats are often seen on the Mount Evans Road.

Picnic
There are very few pullouts on the narrow, winding Mount Evans Road. The best places for picnic stops are the parking lots at Mount Goliath Natural Area and Summit Lake Park, and the Mount Evans summit parking lot.

Hiking
Just about all ages and abilities can enjoy the 1/2 mile trail from the Summit Lake parking lot to the overlook of the Chicago Lakes basin. Be prepared for cold, blustery weather at any time during the summer. Serious hikers will enjoy the two mile hike to the summit of Mount Evans from the Chicago Lakes overlook. Overnight backpackers can take the Summit Lake Trail east from the parking lot all the way to Camp Rock in the Mount Evans State Wildlife Area (map page 116).

Biking
Cycling is increasingly popular on the Mount Evans Road, however due to the extreme narrowness of the road, cyclists and drivers alike should use extreme caution.

Wildlife Viewing
Look for elk in the meadows prior to Summit Lake, and for bighorn sheep in the rocky area just before the summit.

Getaway 22- Winter Park

Getting There-
Winter Park is 67 miles northwest of Denver. Take I-70 west to the exit for Highway 40, and then drive northwest over Berthoud Pass to Winter Park.

The Story Behind The Park
With the grand opening of the Moffat Tunnel on February 26, 1928, train riders at the West Portal were greeted with scenes of snow-capped mountains and broad valleys. It didn't take long for skiers to discover this new haven of powder. In 1928 Graeme McGowan of Denver, a skier and consultant to the U.S. Forest Service, built a small lodge there for his skier friends (all members of the Colorado Mountain Club). They called their ski group the "Arlberg Club," after the new "Arlberg" technique of downhill skiing, a style named after the town of Arlberg, Austria. Only 12 years later in 1940, the first ski lift was installed and Winter Park opened for business.

Winter Park was 30 years old in 1970, and celebrated with this snow sculpture at the base.

121

George Cranmer, the visionary of Red Rocks Amphitheatre, and Director of Denver's Parks and Improvements Department, was also a dedicated skier. He engineered the purchase of 88.9 acres for Denver at the base of the Grand County mountain in 1939. Seeking funds to construct ski trails and lifts, he approached his wealthy friends in the Denver Country Club for contributions. Cranmer also enlisted volunteer help from members of the Civilian Conservation Corps, the Colorado Mountain Club, and the Arlberg Club to help cut trees and build trails. When construction was finished, Winter Park opened on January 28, 1940 with $1.00 lift tickets to three ski runs served by a T-bar lift. The run at the top of the mountain was named "Cranmer" in honor of Winter Park's most enthusiastic supporter.

In 1970, the Comet T-Bar on the left served more advanced skiers, while novices rode the chairlift to the right.

While Winter Park is a park in the mountains owned by Denver, it has never been administered by the Denver Mountain Parks system. In 1950, Denver ceded operation of its ski area to the Winter Park Recreation Association. This continued until 2003, when Denver and the Winter Park Recreation Association entered into a long-term lease with IntraWest Corporation through 2078 to manage the ski area.

1970 Winter Park 30th Anniversary lift ticket.

Over the years, Winter Park has grown from the single T-bar lift to a huge ski area of 3,078 acres (Denver still only owns 88.9 acres) with 142 designated trails served by 25 lifts. The first major expansion was in 1975, when the Mary Jane area opened south of the Winter Park base. Mary Jane was named after a nearby mine, which in turn was supposedly named after one of the area's early "sporting" women. In 1986, Mary Jane's Backside was opened, when skiers were allowed to go over the crest of the mountain to explore the powder glades and steep slopes without benefit of a lift back up. Skiers had to ski all the way back down to the Mary Jane base on Corona Way to reach a lift back to the top. Later expansion occurred in Parsenn Bowl and Vasquez Ridge.

Panoramic view of Winter Park from the trail to Rogers Pass. Mary Jane area is on the left, and the original Winter Park ski trails are on the right.

By 2003, it was apparent that Winter Park was falling far behind other Colorado ski areas in lodging, facilities and lifts, and that the Winter Park Recreation Association would not be able to provide the modern amenities skiers desired. That's when Denver and the Recreation Association agreed to the management lease with IntraWest Corporation. IntraWest was given permission in the lease to develop lodging facilities at the base, and develop other facilities needed to make Winter Park a world-class ski area that could compete with other resorts. In return for control and management of the ski area for profit, IntraWest agreed to pay Denver Parks $2 million per year, which would go toward capital improvements in city parks, including about $200,000 per year for the Mountain Parks. From 2012 on, the lease returns even larger sums to Denver, as the $2 million per year will be supplemented with a payment of 3% of any gross revenue over $33 million per year. _____

The Winter Park Ski Train

In 1902 David Moffat founded the Denver, Northwestern and Pacific Railway, to link Denver with Salt Lake City. By 1907 rails were extended over Rollins Pass at 11,660 feet elevation, all the way west to Kremmling. The DNW & P was soon spending as much as 40% of its entire annual budget on snowplowing operations on Rollins Pass. To circumvent the high pass and its costs, Moffat dreamed of a tunnel under the mountains west of Denver. Moffat died in 1911 however, long before his dream was fulfilled. In 1913, his railroad emerged as the Denver & Salt Lake Railroad under the direction of Denver financier Charles Boettcher (see page 53).

The Moffat Tunnel was finally built from 1923-1927 at a cost of $18 million and 28 lives lost during construction. The 6.2 mile long tunnel immediately opened the area west of the tunnel to skiing activities, and public demand soon led to passenger trains specifically designated for winter runs. The first official "ski train" ran on the Denver & Salt Lake Railroad on Sunday, February 9, 1936. The Denver Rocky Mountain News sponsored the train and publicized it highly in the newspaper. Over 2,000 tickets were sold, and the train hauled passengers out to the 25th Annual U.S. Western Ski Tournament and Winter Sports Carnival at Hot Sulphur Springs (about 30 miles northwest of Winter Park.)

The Rocky Mountain News continued to sponsor a snow train to Hot Sulphur Springs through 1941, and then abandoned the project as World War II intervened. Meanwhile, the Winter Park Ski Area had opened in 1940, and when the war was over, there was demand for the train to stop there to let skiers off. On April 11, 1947 the Denver & Salt Lake Railroad became part of the Denver & Rio Grande Western Railroad. Later in 1947, the D & RGW agreed to stop the train just west of the West Portal of the Moffat Tunnel to let skiers depart at Winter Park. The Ski Train tradition continued until the last train ran on March 29, 2009.

On March 28, 1987, the Rocky Mountain Railroad Club chartered the Silver Sky dome car and attached it to the end of the Ski Train. The passenger cars in front of the Silver Sky were the old Northern Pacific cars which were then 72 years old. This was their last year on the Ski Train, as they were sold to the Napa Valley Wine Train, and replaced in 1988 with newer cars purchased from VIA Rail in Canada.

Rocky Mountain Railroad Club

SILVER SKY EXCURSION
D&RGW WINTER PARK SKI TRAIN
SATURDAY, MARCH 28, 1987

President, R.M.R.R.C.

Departs Denver
Union Station
7:30 A.M. MST

No. 1

March 28, 1987 the Silver sky was ready for departure at 7:30 a.m. at Denver Union Station on the tail end of the Winter Park Ski Train.

Two hours later, the Silver Sky was parked at the end of the Ski Train, just outside the west portal of the Moffat Tunnel at Winter Park.

127

Turned on the wye at Tabernash, the Ski Train is ready to head back to Denver on March 28, 1987.

Denver oilman, industrialist and financier Philip Anschutz purchased the D& RGW in November of 1984. The heyday of the Ski Train had been in 1966, when the train reached a pinnacle of 22 cars. After that, it began a slow decline as the old cars continued to deteriorate to the point where they were limited to 30 mph in 1987. Anschutz, a rail buff, was determined to return the Ski Train to its glory days. He purchased the VIA Rail cars and sold the old cars. The new cars featured modern seating, snack bars, and served wine and beer. The Ski Train increased in popularity, and made regular runs on Saturdays and Sundays to Winter Park from Christmas week to the first weekend in April. Costs continued to increase for the Ski Train though, and by the turn of the century it was losing money. Anschutz reluctantly decided to sell the train, and the last run of the Ski Train was March 29, 2009.

The Ski Train cars were sold on April 21, 2009 to the Algoma Central Railway in Canada, and on May 8, 2009 the equipment was moved back to Canada from whence it had originally come. In 2010, the San Luis and Rio Grande Railroad (owned by Iowa Pacific Holdings) tried to revive the Ski Train. Equipment was procured and advance tickets were sold. Then the railroad ran into the brick wall known as liability insurance and Amtrak. Disagreement with Amtrak over the amount of insurance and number of Amtrak crew members required to operate the Ski Train, forced Iowa Pacific to cancel the Ski Train. As of 2012, the future looks bleak for ever having a Ski Train to Winter Park again. Fond memories of the Ski Train still linger with those of us fortunate enough to have taken a ride on the grand old train.

Skiers line up for the return trip to Denver on the Winter Park Ski Train on March 28, 1987.

What To Do In The Park- Summer

Scenic Chairlift Ride To Hiking and Biking
Ride the chairlift up the mountain, and spend the day hiking or biking on the mountainside trails.

Alpine Slide
Take the kids (old and young) for a ride down the alpine slide. Ride the chairlift up to the departure point for the slide.

Disc Golf
Ride the chairlift up to the disc golf course, and enjoy a challenging 18-hole disc golf layout on the mountainside.

Concerts
Go to www.winterparkresort.com/events for a list of concerts held during the summer months.

What To Do In The Park- Winter

Downhill Skiing & Snowboarding
Enjoy world-class skiing on Winter Park's 2,886 acres served by 24 lifts. Ski school is available for skiers of all ages and abilities.

Cross Country Skiing And Snowshoeing
Hit the trails on your own, or go with an expert guide.

Ice Skating
Skating is available at the outdoor rink in the Village during ski season.

Sledding And Tubing
Bring your own, or pick up a rental at the park.

Snow Cat Tours
Enjoy an enclosed, heated ride in a 13-passenger snow cat, which will take you to scenic spots across the mountain.

Denver Mountain Parks: Challenges And Hopes For The Future

Denver Mountain Parks have not been adequately funded since the 0.5 mill levy expired in 1956. That translates to over 50 years of deferred maintenance and inadequate protection for the parks. The results are painfully visible- an overturned trash barrel with garbage scattered at Turkey Creek Park; graffiti spray-painted on rocks at Colorow Point Park. Many parks lack signage and are difficult to find. There are no maps, no visitor centers, no informative brochures. There is only one ranger for a 14,000 acre system. Ten employees and a few seasonal employees cover this vast system, barely keeping up with trash pickup, let alone maintenance of buildings and resources.

It is estimated that if the 0.5 mill levy were in effect today, it would raise $4.2 million annually for the Mountain Parks. Instead, the Mountain Parks limp along on an annual budget of barely $1 million- about $200,000 of capital improvement funds and roughly $800,000 from the Parks and Recreation operating budget. Shamefully, this represents only 1% of Denver Parks and Recreation's operating budget. The 2008 Denver Mountain Parks Master Plan estimates that there are currently $23 million in deferred maintenance projects in the Mountain Parks. Some have suggested that Denver sell the mountain parks. Is that really what Denver wants to do with its heritage? And besides, deed restrictions with the U.S. Forest Service state that the land reverts back to the Forest Service at no cost if Denver tries to sell the land or use it for other than park purposes.

The value of Denver Mountain Parks is undeniable. It is not an exaggeration to state that the only mountain ridges west of Denver today that are not dotted with houses, are those which belong to Denver Mountain Parks. Political willpower on the part of Denver government is needed to secure adequate funding for Denver Mountain Parks. Much more of the annual payment from Winter Park must be channeled to the Mountain Parks, as must a greater portion of Parks and Recreation's operating budget. Cooperation from surrounding counties has helped maintain Denver Mountain Parks. Denver must now step up to the plate to ensure spending adequate to maintain these mountain treasures for the next one hundred years.

Bibliography

Albi, Charles and Kenton Forrest. The Moffat Tunnel: A Brief History. Golden, CO: Colorado Railroad Museum, 1984.

Appleby, Susan Consola. Fading Past: the Story of Douglas County Colorado. Palmer Lake, CO: Filter Press, 2001.

Arps, Louisa Ward. Denver In Slices. Athens, OH: Swallow Press, 1983.

Baird, Susan. Denver Mountain Parks Master Plan. Denver, CO: Denver Parks and Recreation, 2008.

Crain, Mary Helen. A Circle of Pioneers. Evergreen, CO: Canyon Courier, 1959.

Downing, Warwick M. "How Denver Acquired Her Celebrated Mountain Parks," in Denver Municipal Facts March-April, 1931.

Friesen, Steve. Buffalo Bill: Scout, Showman, Visionary. Golden, CO: Fulcrum Publishing, 2010.

Home, R. W. "Martin, Florence (1867-1957)" in Australian Dictionary of Biography Volume 10. Canberra, Australia: Australian National University, 1986.

Lomond, Carole. Jefferson County Colorado: A Unique and Eventful History. Golden, CO: Views Publishing Co., 2009.

Matthews, Vincent and Katie KellerLynn and Betty Fox. Messages in Stone: Colorado's Colorful Geology. Denver, CO: Colorado Geological Survey, 2003.

Meyers, Charlie. Colorado Ski Country. Helena, MT: Falcon Press, 1987.

Noel, Thomas J. Sacred Stones: Colorado's Red Rocks Park & Amphitheatre. Denver, CO: City and County of Denver, Division of Theatres and Arenas, 2004.

Noel, Thomas J. and G. Brown with George Krieger. Red Rocks: From Dinosaurs to Rock 'N Roll. Denver, CO: City and County of Denver, Division of Theatres and Arenas, 2003.

Noel, Thomas J. and Barbara S. Norgren. Denver The City Beautiful. Denver, CO: Historic Denver Inc., 1987.

Noel, Thomas J. and Stephen J. Leonard. Denver Mining Camp to Metropolis. Niwot, CO: University Press of Colorado, 1990.

Noel, Thomas J. (introduction). The WPA Guide to 1930s Colorado. Lawrence, KS: University Press of Kansas, 1987.

Noel, Thomas J. Buildings of Colorado. New York, NY: Oxford University Press, 1997.

Norman, Reuben O. The Blue Book: The Who's Who of Denver, 1931-1932. Denver, CO: The Blue Book Company, 1931.

Patterson, Steve and Kenton Forrest. The Ski Train. Golden, CO: Colorado Railroad Museum, 1995.

Robertson, Janet Neuhoff, et.al. 100 Years Up High: Colorado Mountains and Mountaineers. Golden, CO: Colorado Mountain Club Press, 2011

About The Author

Mike Butler retired as Manager for the Denver Parks administration office, where he worked with Denver city and mountain parks superintendents. A graduate of the University of Nebraska, he was trained in history, geography, and education. He is the author of Around the Spanish Peaks (Arcadia Publishing, 2012), and Great Sand Dunes National Park (Arcadia Publishing, 2013). He traveled to all 22 developed Denver Mountain Parks to research this book. He currently lives in Highlands Ranch, Colorado.

www.ingramcontent.com/pod-product-compliance
Lightning Source LLC
LaVergne TN
LVHW021511080426
835509LV00018B/2483